Greek Ph

CW01508117

The Lives And '
Plato And Aristotle

By Simon T. Bailey

Table of Contents

INTRODUCTION: THE PHILOSOPHERS OF ATHENS' GOLDEN AGE

Echoes from Athens' golden days still reach those of us willing to forsake our high-speed computers and steady streams of overstimulation to stand patiently for a moment and look around. A warm breeze curls around your neck. Is the smell of burning flesh the product of a nearby street vendor, or is it the leftover sacrifices to Athena that happened on this spot 2400 years ago? Reason tells us it's the former. But what if we can let our imaginations run away for a moment?

The ruins of the ancient days are sprinkled over the landscape of the modern city as if they are skeletons trying to climb out of closets in order to tell us their stories. It's easy to rush by them. After all, as ancient as it is, Athens is a modern city, and like most modern cities, it had forged ahead with making a new future for itself.

Businesspeople on cell phones speak in rapid Greek. Vendors sell cheap t-shirts and post cards. Tourists call to their children who are trying to climb through the fence rails that close off bits of history.

Some of Athens' people realize how strange it is that they are alive and walking through the same stomping grounds that some of the greatest minds in human history walked through two and a half millennia ago, at the end of Greece's Golden Age, when Socrates was tried and condemned to death for impiety and corrupting the youth, when Plato preserved Socrates' teachings in his dialogues and founded the Academy, and when Aristotle created the beginning of the scientific method and founded the Academy's biggest competitor, the Lyceum.

Athens was one of the biggest Greek city-states of the time, likely supporting about 350,000 inhabitants around 430 BCE. It was the city of the patron goddess, Athena. Most of its food was obtained through commerce across the Black Sea, which became a problem when Athens went to war against Sparta, as once the supply line was cut off, the Athenians could be starved into submission.

Due to geography, there was very little land for farmers to pass on to their children, little natural food supply, and little ability for population growth in the city itself. This caused conflict among those without land. Sometimes, these conflicts were resolved through uprisings followed by constitutional rewrites, and sometimes they were solved by sending some of the landless population to form a daughter city, which would be politically, but not economically, connected to Athens.

Persia often interfered in the politics of the Greek city-states when it suited, though Persia's interference wasn't necessarily needed for the conflicts between rivals Sparta and Athens to flourish on their own. While Athens experienced a Golden Age after the Persian War with the rebuilding of the Acropolis and a blossoming of the arts, Sparta stuck to its regimented tradition of military preparedness.

As city-states formed alliances with either Athens or Sparta, they lost much of what had made them culturally distinctive entities, adopting governments and military tactics, and eventually religious and social customs. The city of Athena was not immune from losing its uniqueness. It became more and more cosmopolitan, allowing aliens from all over Greece to move there to live. These aliens brought their own customs, languages, and gods, making Athens into a melting pot of diversity.

In many ways, the fourth and fifth centuries weren't so different from our own. The baseline of human nature doesn't seem to have changed. People today are just as eager to be successful in love and business, wealth and war, religion and eternity. People today still listen to stories about heroes and want to emulate them. We still care about asserting our opinions and having our way.

But despite our similarities, it would be a mistake to assume that we are too similar when it comes to our ideologies. A mistake that modern scholars make occurs in trying to pinpoint where in our own agendas and political leanings the great Greek philosophers would have fallen. Were the classical philosophers utopian, dystopian, egalitarian, liberal, anarchic, democratic, oligarchic, dictatorial, monarchic, or republican? Were they some combination of our own categories?

Democracy in Athens was very different from democracy in the United States of America. Citizens who possessed a certain amount of property were allowed to vote directly on legislations. Leaders who took care of the various state functions were elected or chosen by lot from among the thousands of qualified citizens. Citizenship, however, was not merely granted to everyone born in Athens. Only men could become citizens, as women were little better than property. Often citizenship was offered as an award for heroic deeds or granted as the lucky result of knowing the right combination of officials.

Unlike us, the Athenians in government didn't debate issues like women's rights, slavery, homosexuality, weapon control, education, and equal opportunities for all races, religions, genders, and ethnicities. Equality only applied to men who were citizens, slavery was taken for granted, sexual orientation wasn't a thing, and education was not an issue that the government dealt with.

Trying to fit Socrates, Plato, and Aristotle into our own schemas is a natural human inclination, but in so doing, we risk limiting what we are able to learn from them and their teachings.

In a similar way, it's tempting to read the writings and teachings of these philosophers and draw links to their lives, despite having no evidence that such links are warranted. Wanting a literary plot to exist is natural. As humans, we want our own lives to have a meaningful plot, and we expect that the great figures of our past should have the same.

However, it's important to understand while reading this book that very little in the line of plot or actual historical data exists about the lives of Socrates, Plato, and Aristotle. Ancient historians cared much more about preserving the philosophy than the life stories of the philosophers, so we only know of a few sketchy events, and many of them are conjectures based on what historians know of what was going on in the world at the time.

If we can't make much more than a basic timeline of their lives, what, then, is the point of this book? This book seeks to bring to life the possibilities of the western world's most enduring philosophers and answer contextual questions that will bring their teachings and writings to life in a whole new way.

What was Athens like in the fifth and fourth centuries BCE? What was the political climate like? What was the class structure? What lasting impact did the war against Sparta have? Did the Greeks truly condone pedophilia? What rights did women have? How did the philosophers' views differ from the general publics' ideologies? What did democracy mean to them? And, most of all, what did it mean to be human?

This book is not meant as a substitute for reading the philosophers' work for yourself; it is meant to give you a context with which to more fully understand their work. That said, you should absolutely still read Plato's dialogues and Aristotle's lectures notes. There is no substitute for them. No summary does them justice.

Because there are already many commentaries out there on the Greek philosophers, rather than taking the dry tone of many of these commentaries, which certainly serve their purpose, this book seeks to take a more user-friendly approach. Important events from the philosophers' lives have been dramatized in a fictional style to give you a more immediate feel for what it might have been like for them to be human in the fourth and fifth centuries.

I am not a "real" historian in the sense that I haven't written this as a giant dissertation that second guesses its every statement in stuffy, tired academic prose. If you are looking for the cold, hard facts and nothing further, then this isn't the book for you. If you are looking for a treatise on the intricate workings of the Greek philosophers' inner minds and most complex thoughts, then this book isn't what you're looking for. If you're looking for a traditional commentary, then this book won't fit the bill.

If, however, you are thinking about getting into philosophy and want something easy to start out with, then this is the book for you. If you've tried to read Plato or Aristotle but found yourself mystified on one page one, then this book is a great jumping off point. If you've been reading Plato or Aristotle and find yourself wondering at what the point of any of it is, then this book can show you the human side of philosophy and bring to life some of the challenges the philosophers faced in their day as they went about their lives and teachings in classical Athens.

CHAPTER ONE: SOCTRATES' TRIAL AND THE FREEDOM OF SPEECH

May, 399 BCE, Athens

Whispers and shuffles echoed through the cavernous marble courtroom. Somewhere in the room a man laughed and was hushed quickly by his companion. People continued to enter, eager to witness the biggest public spectacle of the year—perhaps of the century. They weren't just Athenians. Many of them came from surrounding city-states outside of the eastern peninsula of Attica.

The man on trial stood at the front of the hall, partially obstructing himself with a marble pillar. He was a short, pudgy old man with a craggy beard, wide set eyes, and large nostrils. He wore a threadbare himation wrapped in folds over his body. He stared into the crowd, letting his gaze sweep from one side of the room to the other and slowing over the faces of the five hundred jury members, called *dikasts*, who had been chosen by lot from among the Athenian citizens. The vast number of jury members was meant to make it difficult for the convicted to bribe enough of them to swing the vote in his favor.

Socrates almost laughed. Even if he had been inclined to pay off the jury for an acquittal, he was as poor as the cloth on his body. These were the men who would determine Socrates' fate by a majority vote.

Freedom of speech in Athens was limited only by a man's ability to defend himself in court. Popular plays of the day by Aristophanes did everything from portray bodily functions to blatantly skewer local celebrities. A man could say what he wanted as long as he could put on a sympathetic show in front of the court.

"I heard he waddles like a duck," a young man whispered to his companion.

His companion whispered back, "I heard he's as ugly as Silenus." Silenus was the leader of the mythical satyrs, grotesque beings that were part goat and part human.

The old man, Socrates, stepped from behind his pillar, and the crowd hushed.

The charges, brought against him were spoken by Meletus, a long-haired, hook-nosed man with a thin, scraggly beard. Socrates was being charged with corrupting the minds of the youth with his teachings and encouraging them to disrespect their parents and their country. He was charged also with two counts of impiety. He was accused both of not believing in Zeus and Hera and their companions and of trying to introduce new gods to Athens.

The charges were vague enough to be convincing but hid Socrates' real crimes, which consisted of associating with traitors, criticizing democracy, and failing to speak out against the rule of the thirty tyrants back in 404 and 403 BCE after Sparta had beat Athens in the

Peloponnesian War and installed its own oligarchic government in Athens. Amnesty laws had been passed, however, prohibiting punishments for any crimes committed under the Thirty Tyrants. Events from those times could not legally be mentioned, so Meletus had had to get creative to bring Socrates to court, and he'd done a good job. Impiety was a capital crime, and the Athenians would not look upon it lightly.

Socrates knew all of this.

He took a deep breath and willed his hands to stop their shaking. He already knew how this would end, but he refused to show fear or cowardice. He knew that Meletus would call for his execution and felt fairly certain that it would be the jury's choice as well, because he did not intend to grovel or stoop to the rhetoric of the Sophists in order to go free. If a man couldn't defend his values even in the face of death, then *he* was either too weak or his values were too weak. Socrates knew that his values were not too weak.

Besides, death could not possibly be the worst punishment for an old man living in poverty. He was seventy years old and the son of a stonemason and a midwife. He had no wealth, no connections, and, soon enough, his health would fail, causing him to live out his days in the misery known only to the elderly living in poverty. Pain did not mix well with poorness. He blinked hard, rolling his eyes as he opened them. It was ridiculous, really, yet here he was.

Meletus called Anytus and Lycon, who was a professional orator, as witnesses to testify against him.

445 BCE, Outskirts of the Agora, Athens

Young Socrates ran along the market at the southwest corner of Athens' Agora. He wasn't yet old enough to enter the Agora. Only grown male citizens could enter into the bustle of gossip and politics and philosophy being discussed there in the city center. Busts of Hermes guarded the line that young people and women were never to cross.

Socrates paused for a moment, looking in on the tall roof of the stoa he could see rising above its neighboring buildings from where he stood. The stoa was one of the largest in Athens. The roof pointed, and columns fell from the base of the roof in a long colonnade. He couldn't see the ground it rested on, but he could imagine it, and someday, he knew, he wouldn't have to imagine. He would be in that stoa talking about philosophy with the wisest and most important men in Athens.

He picked up his pace. His friend, Simon, was expecting him.

Simon's shop greeted him, as plain at the Agora was elegant. It was shaded by canvas and sported shoes of varying shapes and sizes. There were elegant strappy sandals and thick sturdy ones, and the whole place smelled of leather.

Socrates walked inside, wondering if Simon had made a decision.

A couple of men stood talking with Simon, and Socrates wandered the shop looking at the items there for what must have been the thousandth time. It was in this small shop that Socrates had learned to love debating all manner of subjects, whether it was love, jealousy, or the role of goodness in society.

Pots of hobnails stood on a worktable at the back of the shop. He ran his finger along the letters carved into a ceramic drinking mug. "Simon," it said. Various metal tools were set neatly along the sides of the table, including a few forms that Simon used to fit the shoe leather around to get the right size and shape of the shoe.

After years of watching Simon make shoes, Socrates was finally starting to make shoes himself. He wasn't the craftsman Simon was, but he could make a simple, sturdy shoe without much supervision.

A hint of a breeze filtered through the wide front entrance to the shop, spilling the late morning sunshine in with it. The men talking with Simon gave him some coins and left the shop.

Simon turned to Socrates.

"What did you decide?" Socrates asked.

Last week, the well-known orator, statesman, and general, Pericles, had offered Simon residence in his own home. Simon was becoming known for his philosophizing. His work as a cobbler kept up his expenses, but philosophy was his love. Taking Pericles' offer would allow him to focus on his philosophizing and writing. Socrates would be sad to see this little shop and Simon's house attached to it vacated and then taken by a stranger, but he would be happy that Simon would finally have the patronage he deserved.

"I turned him down," Simon said.

Socrates shook his head quickly, unsure if he'd misheard. "What?"

"I can't take the offer." Simon sat at his worktable and picked up the shoe he was working on. "I could no longer call myself a free man if I went to live with Pericles."

"You don't mean that he would make you a slave," Socrates said. Pericles was known to be a fair man and a noble warrior.

"Not in a manner of speaking," Simon said. "But to take such a payment from him would put me in his debt and swear my loyalty to him regardless of how I personally feel about his actions. I'm mean, he recently divorced his wife, and rumor has it that he's taken a foreign mistress, a woman by the name of Aspasia of Miletus."

"I've heard the name," Socrates said. "Isn't she a hetaera?"

"Yes. She runs a brothel in the city," Simon said. "A very forward, indecent woman."

A hetaera was different from other Athenian women. She was not respectable among the other women, and, Socrates imagined, her differences in profession and education gave her little in common with respectable women anyway. Hetaerae were professional entertainers, courtesans, or companions. They were usually very well educated, independent, and required to pay taxes.

"What do you know of her?" Socrates asked, fascinated by the idea of an educated woman.

"I've heard that she'd an excellent conversationalist and that despite the immoral ways in which she chooses to live, men still like to go and hear her converse. Some of them bring their wives along." Simon removed the form from inside the shoe. "If I had accepted Pericles as my patron, I would have been obligated to agree with his decisions and actively support his indiscretions and politics, regardless of the law and the truth."

Socrates nodded. It shouldn't come as such a shock to him, really. Simon was fiercely independent, and that independence made him able to think and speak freely in a way that he might not have been able to have otherwise.

"Freedom of speech once bought and paid for is no longer free," Simon said.

339 BCE

Anytus and Lycon took their places in the courtroom after their speeches. Socrates had paid as little attention to them as he could justify, knowing that he would be cross-examining each of them later.

He chose to put most of his focus on what he knew he had to say to the jury and to the crowds gathered here as if they had come to a great theater production. Looking out upon them, he saw the interest and suspense in their faces that came from not knowing how this trial would end.

What he had to say wouldn't persuade the jury not to convict him, but it was necessary for the city of Athens to hear the truth. He was willing to be the gadfly, the sting that Athens needed to wake up and right its wrongs. The times were difficult, and Athens needed a scapegoat. Perhaps once he was gone, the city of Athens would see where it had gone wrong.

As the cold of the marble floor crept up his legs, Socrates took another deep breath. This would be his last stand, and he would make the most of it, assuming that his fate was already sealed. "How you felt, gentlemen, when you heard my accusers, I do not know..."

He made the argument that he was not an eloquent speaker unless eloquence could be defined as the mere force of truth. Then, he listed his accusers, those being Meletus, Anytus, and Lycon, along with those who were like shadows because they could not be brought to court and cross examined—all of those who slandered him and distorted his ideas.

The shadows would be hardest to defend against.

CHAPTER TWO: THE ORACLE OF DELPHI

335 BCE, Delphi

Socrates' impetuous friend, Chaerephon, traveled to the sacred harbor of Kirrha, which was where the most sacred site in the Greek world resided. When the sun slanted over the horizon in the mornings and evenings, pink veins reached from the depths of Mount Parnassus. In the daytime, the granite mountain turned white with the heat of Apollo.

Legend had it that at the beginning of time, Zeus had released two eagles. One flew east, and the other flew west until they met at earth's belly button, the center of the world, and the spiritual center of the universe. This legend was far older than the Greeks, and by Socrates' time, even the Greeks believed that by traveling to Delphi to speak with the oracle, one could have any question they asked answered by Apollo himself.

It was with this in mind that Chaerephon docked at Kirrha, made his purchases on the bustling shoreline marketplace, and began the steep climb up Mount Parnassus to Delphi to question the oracle regarding the wisest man in the world.

Delphi was tucked into the mountains at a place called "The Shining Ones." Its streets were slick from the feet of men and made of the same stone as the mountain. Roads and buildings alike looked like they were on loan from the mountain and could at any point disappear, sinking back into the mountain from which they came.

Chaerephon washed himself in the holy Kastalian spring. The water was cold and pure. Once purified, he pushed his way through the sojourning crowds up the Sacred Way, mindful of the colossal sphinx and the great statue of Apollo along with the stores of war booty that had been dedicated as per the requirement upon victory.

Chaerephon walked into Apollo's sanctuary and offered the ritual sacrifice on the altar there. He entered the inner sanctum full of nervous, expectant energy. The Pythia, which was the voice of the oracle, was there.

The room smelled of burnt flesh, laurel leaves, barley, and flames. Hallucinogenic gases emanated from a crack in the ground where two fault lines met and spewed ethylene and other hydrocarbon gases into the air. The room's walls were carved with aphorisms. "Know yourself," one of them read. "Nothing in excess," read another.

Chaerephon knelt and asked the question that would haunt Socrates until the day he died. "Is there any man wiser than Socrates?"

The oracle babbled, and the priestess translated the answer, as was the custom: "No."

Chaerephon brought the oracle's confirmation back to Socrates, who was incredulous.

"Certainly there are wiser men than I," Socrates said. Could the oracle have been mistaken?

399 BCE

Socrates stood before the jury, the audience, and his accusers. Some of them had heard a version of the oracle's proclamation about Socrates. The oracle of Delphi was, to many of them, irrefutable, though there were some who would argue that the oracle had been wrong about some of the outcomes of the Persian War for some mystical reason that only Apollo could know. Thus, the oracle could also be wrong about Socrates as well. Or perhaps the oracle's words had been misinterpreted. Socrates saw the skepticism in their eyes and slid his gaze to that of young Plato, whose belief in him, he knew, was steadfast.

Socrates continued, "After giving me the oracle's answer, Chaerephon looked at me, unspeaking. He had nothing further to say on the matter. The oracle had spoken.

"Like many of you, I was incredulous. I became determined to disprove the oracle's statement. I visited the men reputed to be among the wisest in Athens. I questioned them closely, finding that the men who claimed to be the wisest had arguments and rhetoric that fell apart under the most insignificant lines of questioning.

"Paradoxically, I found that the men who claimed to know the most were the men who, in actuality, seemed to know the least. Those most confident of their knowledge were the easiest to strip of that knowledge. I discovered no proof that the oracle was wrong about me, and I could only deduce that what made me the wisest man in the world was the fact that, unlike the world's most important men, I made no claims of knowing anything.

"I think what the oracle meant by saying that I was the wisest of men was that only God is wise, and that the wisest of men are those who acknowledge that their wisdom is worth nothing by comparison."

Plato nodded eagerly at the old man. A murmur trickled through the crowd, but a glance at the jury revealed that while a few of them nodded in understanding, most of them stared stonily at him, determined that his accusations should stick. He had known and questioned many of them at one point or another in the Agora. He'd boldly embarrassed many of them with his questions and revealed to them their fallacious thinking. As much as he'd like to believe that they would realize that he was doing them a service, and as much as he'd like to believe that their embarrassment and anger wouldn't cloud their decision about his conviction, he knew that even a democracy ruled by the people could not keep out the same human biases of all other forms of government.

The Athenian Agora, Some Years Earlier

The Agora was full of the objects of a religious community. Merchants' stalls sold portable shrines for individual households. Sanctuaries were built messily all over the Agora streets for men to bring sacrifices. The sanctuaries smelled of dove blood and burnt goat fur and were surrounded by clay jars of diseased limbs, knees, eyes, and genitalia. A greasy haze of smoke pooled around the sacrifice areas from the sacrifices that happened all day long.

The Athenians were a deeply religious people whose religious practices were as integral to their daily lives as eating and drinking. They worshipped any number of gods at any given time out of a fear that their lives hung in the hands of fickle otherworldly beings who could strike them down with disease or destroy their crops on a whim if they failed to pay their dues at the proper time.

These gods were not concerned with having personal relationships with their subjects. A man didn't practice his religion personally and individually, but as a corporate act. Worship and sacrifice was always done as a community.

Temples and shrines to Aphrodite, Hephaestus, Zeus, and any number of other demigods were sprinkled within the cacophony of the Agora's marketplace and government buildings. Soldiers could be heard drilling for battle in the distance in order to defend this great city.

Over the whole Agora stood Athena's Parthenon up in the acropolis looking down on all of Athens.

Men came to the Agora for discussion, business, politics, and religion. More gossip was exchanged under the eaves of the government stoas than anywhere else in the city. By mid morning, the Agora was bustling with the day's activities. Slaves cleaned the feces of animals from the streets, while eerily lifelike bronze statues followed their movements with dead eyes.

Eastern spices and southern saffron mingled with the smell of human sweat from slaves being driven to the market to trade. These were familiar sights and scents to Socrates.

Socrates was known as a busybody who was prone to accosting men in the streets to ask them any number of odd philosophical questions. One afternoon, he popped out from the wide shelter of a stoa into the path of young man by the name of Xenophon.

"I have a list of things I'm looking for," Socrates said to the young man. "Would you help me?"

Xenophon nodded, fascinated with the eccentric old man he'd heard bits of gossip about. He had heard tell that Socrates had a tendency to pause in his speech and stare off into space for a few minutes or hours without being aware of what was going on around him. Some said that he'd been touched by the gods. Others said that he was simply crazy. Whichever the case might be, Socrates was one of the most interesting characters to roam the Agora streets.

Socrates went on to list a series of mundane household items. Xenophon told him where he could find each object in turn. Last on the list, Socrates asked, "And what about a brave and virtuous man?"

Xenophon paused, thrown off from the drastic change from household objects to the abstraction of virtue. "I'm not sure I know what you mean," he said to the older man.

Socrates nodded at him and indicated that he should follow him. "Come with me. Let's see what you might learn."

From that day on, Xenophon followed the strange man, meeting him along with other followers in the Agora to discuss what it meant to be a virtuous man, along with a vast array of other subjects. Among Socrates' other followers was a young Plato.

Socrates employed a peculiar method of teaching in which he pretended to know nothing and questioned people about subjects like beauty and goodness in order to get to the root of peoples' beliefs. While he humiliated and annoyed many people with his impossible questions, his eccentricities and questions weren't the ultimate reason why he was accused and brought to trial for capital punishment.

In fact, the reasons given for his arrest, trial, and subsequent execution were, perhaps, the few reasons for which Socrates could claim no guilt.

CHAPTER THREE: SOCRATES AT BATTLE

November, 432 BCE, Potidaea

Socrates' spear grew heavier the longer he carried it. As a hoplite, or citizen soldier, he was armored in bronze and was supposed to move in a phalanx formation as he had been trained. But training was nothing compared with a real battle. They'd been pushed back. He knew he was taking more backward steps than forward, and his spear was hitting more air than flesh.

Potidaea had been founded by the Corinthians in 600 BCE, but now the Corinthians were aligned with the Spartans, while Potidaea held a tenuous alliance with the Athenian League. The Athenians had asked Potidaea to tear down part of its walls and kick out the Corinthian ambassadors as a precaution. They didn't want to lose Potidaea to Sparta, and they didn't want to go to war with Sparta. Everyone knew about the Spartans' reputation as the most ruthless military force in the known world.

There had been some whispers about revolt in Potidaea, and after the near disaster at the Battle of Sybota, they didn't want to take any more chances. Sparta had offered Potidaea help with a revolt against Athens. The Athenians couldn't let that happen.

Adrenaline pressed through Socrates' veins. A giant of a man came at him, his spear aimed directly at Socrates face. Socrates feinted left and dodged right, thrusting his spear hard into the large man and pushing until the man's eyes went glassy and he toppled over backward.

Socrates ripped his spear from the man's middle, wanting to his eyes as the blood pooled up from the fatal wound and fell like a red waterfall down the man's side.

His spear came free in time to swing and hit another enemy. The man tripped dodging Socrates' spear, and Socrates made the plunge.

A familiar scream lit the air.

Socrates jerked his spear free and twisted to see his friend, Alcibiades lying on the ground trying to fend off a couple of Corinthian soldiers. He held his left hand to the place on his side not covered by the armor. His face was white like death. The young aristocrat had shared his tent with Socrates so that he wouldn't be cold out in the open air at night. Tents were a luxury that few but the wealthiest soldiers could afford to have.

Socrates ran the twenty feet to Alcibiades, striking the larger soldier in the side of the neck and quickly recovering to beat off the second man. Another enemy soldier pitted himself in Socrates' path, and Socrates threw his spear into the man's stomach hard enough to crack his armor and wound him badly enough to force him to back down. Socrates removed his knife from its sheath, needing a weapon that would be lighter and faster to wield.

As he leaned to grab the knife, the enemy struck his chest. His armor remained in tact, but the blow knocked the wind out of him and forced him back a few paces. Socrates forced himself to breathe. The air smelled like blood and wet earth. When would this be over? There was no time for the train of thought.

He attacked his pursuer with the weapon in his hand, seeing out the corner of his eye that Alcibiades wasn't moving.

A startling cry went up from the enemy, and suddenly, Corinthian and Potidaean men were retreating.

Socrates put his knife back in its sheath and ran to Alcibiades, dropping down next to the young man's unmoving form. He slapped his friend's face. He had a face far too pretty for his own good. His eyes opened.

"It's not time for death," Socrates said.

"They didn't take my weapons, did they?" Alcibiades asked, the words causing him great effort.

"Your weapons remain," Socrates said. He saw the blood squeezing between the young man's fingers, which were pressed to his side. He tore the fabric of his tunic and stuffed it into the wound. "If I help you stand, can you make it to camp?"

"My armor," Alcibiades said.

Socrates bent and picked up the specially brought bronze armor that bore marks of battle now along with the marks of Alcibiades' noble family lineage.

Alcibiades winced as Socrates wound his arm around the injured man's shoulders and under his arms to help pull him to his feet.

"The enemy is retreating," Socrates said. "You can make it to camp."

Alcibiades winced as he put one foot in front of the other. "You saved my life," he said.

"I did the only thing a friend could do for a friend," Socrates said.

339 BCE

Socrates called the prosecutor, Meletus, to the stand for a cross examination, as the law allowed him to do. Meletus stood before the crowded hall with a smug look on his face. Socrates was a dead man standing. What could he do to Meletus, who had the crowds and the courts on his side?

Socrates faced Meletus. It was time for the biggest battle of his life, and as in hand to hand combat, he would not back down or retreat.

"You've accused me of corrupting the youth," Socrates said.

"That is correct," Meletus said, his voice dripping with sarcasm. "I believe we've already established that fact."

Socrates ignored the tone and the laughter that reverberated off of the stone walls and ceiling all around him and pressed forward. "Do you, Meletus, think that it's important for our youth to be trained in moral excellence?"

"What kind of question is that?" Meletus asked.

Socrates looked at him pointedly.

Meletus, playing to his audience, looked at them with humor and pride. "Of course. I am an upright man."

"Then tell us, Meletus, who makes the young people upright and moral?" Socrates said. "You have gone to all the trouble to figure out who it is who corrupts them and have accused me of being that person. Tell me who makes them moral? You must know."

Meletus froze. He hadn't seen that line of reasoning coming. A baby crying in Sparta could have been heard over the deafening silence that reigned inside the courtroom. Meletus looked from one side of the room to the next, licking his lips nervously.

"You are silent," Socrates said. "It appears that you have not given the matter much thought. It's interesting that you've thought so long and hard over finding and accusing me of being a corrupter when you've given so very little thought to who raises them up in morality. Tell us who makes our young people moral. Speak up."

Meletus sputtered for a moment before resting on the answer that came most quickly to mind. "The laws," he said. "The laws make our young people upright and moral."

"I didn't ask you what. I asked you who. Who makes our youth moral? Which person or people do that?"

Meletus looked around him tensely. Then his face rested, as the go to answer of any prosecutor came to mind. "The jury," He said. "The jurors do."

"There are five hundred of them," Socrates pointed out. "You're saying that all five hundred of them are responsible for teaching morality to young people?"

"Yes, all of them," Meletus said.

Socrates smiled, noting that Meletus visibly relaxed as he gave this answer. The fool. "Then we've got a lot of teachers for our youth. That's certainly a relief."

"Yes, it is," Meletus said, smugly.

"Would you say that the same is true for the audience here today?"

"Of course," Meletus said.

"And the council members as well?"

"Indeed."

"Well then, it would seem that all of Athens is helping to improve our young people. I am the only one who is corrupting them. Is that what you're trying to say?"

"That is precisely what I am trying to say," Meletus said.

"You've checked and I alone am the sole reason why any of our youth are corrupted?"

Meletus frowned. "That is exactly what I'm saying. How many times do you need me to tell you? I emphatically hold that you alone are corrupting the Athenian young people," he snapped.

"And how is it that I am, as you say, corrupting them?"

"You are teaching them to disregard the gods of Athens," Meletus said.

"And I am teaching them to believe in other gods?"

"Yes. Are you deaf? How many times must I tell you?"

A few members of the crowd sniggered. Socrates continued as if he had not heard them. "I don't understand what you mean by this accusation. Do you mean that I teach the youth to believe in gods that Athens doesn't recognize or that I teach them to not believe in gods because I am an atheist?"

"You are an atheist," Meletus said.

"It's interesting that you say that," Socrates said. "Why do you think that?"

"By Zeus, you believe in no gods. You are an atheist."

"I'm quite certain that no one believes you and that you yourself don't even believe you. Men of Athens, doesn't it seem that Meletus is recklessly making claims which he cannot support? He's created quite the riddle for us. First he accuses me of believing in gods other than the gods of Athens and then he accuses me of not believing in gods. Who would believe such convoluted claims? It would be like believing in horses but not in horsemanship or in flutes but not flute players. No one believes claims like those.

"Answer this for me: Can someone believe in spirituality and divinity without believing in spirits or demigods?"

"No, he can't."

"And yet you've accused me of teaching and believing in divine beings other than the ones Athens condones. But if I believe in divine beings, doesn't that necessarily mean that I must believe in spirits and demigods? But you claim that I don't believe in spirits and demigods. Am I teaching that which I don't believe? What benefit does that have for me? How can I be an atheist who believes in gods? Your accusation has no logic. Did you accuse me of such a ridiculous thing because you had nothing else to accuse me of?"

The hall was quiet. Socrates looked out over the audience and the jury. His followers grinned at him, understanding that Meletus had been completely discredited. Socrates nodded at them but inwardly sighed. He could pick apart the illogical nature of the accusations against him for hours, but it would all come to the same thing.

CHAPTER FOUR: THE OLIGARCHY OF THE THIRTY TYRANTS

404 BCE, Athens

Athens, the mighty symbol of democracy and free speech, had been struck down by the gods. Having surrendered to the Spartan general, Lysander, the desolate city was taken over by a council of thirty Athenian citizens who had Spartan or oligarchic political leanings. Perhaps they were lucky to have escaped the total destruction that Sparta usually brought to a conquered city, but the following year of oligarchic rule would call that into question.

Starvation and plague had ravaged the Athenian population in the final years of the Peloponnesian War, slicing a population that had once consisted of 200,000 men in half. By the time the Thirty Tyrants stepped in to rule, the city's inhabitants numbered only 60,000, only half of which were men. About 10,000 of this number lived within the city walls, which had been partially ripped down by the Spartan army.

The council of Thirty released a list of 3,000 citizens who were approved to live in Athens. The lives of everyone else were up for the taking.

Theramenes, one of the Thirty who was certainly not a democrat, thought that this list of 3,000 was too restrictive. He stood before the council and protested against it, and the only thing they changed their mind about was in letting Theramenes live. They executed him by the administration of hemlock poison, which had become a highly perfected art form in the last few years, and it killed him swiftly.

The hemlock treatment had become a popular method of execution. Herbalists had discovered that it only took a quarter of an ounce to kill a person, and sometimes even less. The hemlock plant was skinned, ground with a mortar and pestle, and then run through a sieve to make it into the most effective consistency. It was a cheap and fast weapon to manufacture.

The playwright, Aristophenes commented on how ridiculous it was that men were constantly working out more and more methods of killing each other. The statement was apt.

Desperate Athenians had been pitted against their own friends and family members in the battle of their lives. A hundred men disappeared every month. Some were poisoned or stifled in their beds, and those were the lucky ones. Others were attacked by death squads, brutally beaten, robbed, raped, and killed. Still others were dropped, alive, into pits and buried or drowned. Some were strapped to wooden boards by their necks, arms, and legs with metal cuffs.

Money held no powers of protection. People were as likely to be killed for their money as they were for their politics. A greedy citizen often robbed and killed his neighbor out of a belief that that neighbor was not deserving of the wealth he possessed. Looters dug through carcasses, ripping earrings from the unhearing ears of well-to-do Athenian wives.

Many democratic Athenians managed to escape the nightmare that their beloved city had become, sneaking through the rubble of the destroyed walls and finding refuge together in camps miles outside of the city's perimeter.

Critias, who was formerly a frequent dinner companion of Socrates, was appointed as a member of the Thirty Tyrants. He didn't forget the way Socrates had called him a pig because of the promiscuous ways in which he behaved with other men. He cut Socrates off from the dinner parties, but, mysteriously, Socrates still made the tyrants' list of approved citizens. Even more mysteriously, was Socrates's uncharacteristic silence during this violent time in Athenian history, a silence that would cost him his life a few years later, as he was accused under the tables of having an undemocratic leaning.

Phyle

Three miles northeast of Athens, where pine trees rose along a steep hill and scented the air, Athenian democrats fled in swarms to the settlement of Phyle. In the summer, the residents of Phyle could look for miles across the Greek plains of Attica. In the winter, the clouds wrapped their mists around the settlement and tucked it out of sight from onlookers below it.

Socrates' friend, Chaerephon, stood on the edge of the promontory watching the army of pro-Spartans coming closer. The day was clear and cold. He shivered, whether from fear or cold was unclear, even to him.

The democrats with him up in Phyle had been steadfastly planning to overthrow the Thirty Tyrants, but they were not ready yet, and they had no defense but the steep climb with which to fight the enemy now at the bottom of the hill.

Chaerephon ran to the village center and called to the others. The men gathered around the altar that had been built to the gods. Their wives and a few children gathered in the doorways. "It looks like the only thing that will save us all is a miracle," he said.

"Then we shall have to pray for a miracle," said another of the men.

Most of the others in the group nodded.

"What have we got for weapons?" another asked.

"There are enough spears for most of us, but even if every man and woman fights, we are severely outnumbered," Chaerephon said. He was a thin old man whose skin clung to his bones and squeezed until the blue-green of his veins could be seen. He'd once adventured up to Delphi to ask the Oracle if there was anyone wiser than Socrates. Now, the adventurous spirit had been replaced by a desperation merely to survive.

A bleating rose on the air. One of the younger men seized the last thin goat from the fold and brought it wordlessly forward. No one moved to stop him.

The altar was lit, and the goat was cut open and placed on the altar as cries went up from the people to whichever gods might hear them and take pity.

A snowflake fell on the flames.

The people shivered. Chaerephon ran back to the edge of the cliff to see how far the Tyrants had come. They were now to the foot of the hill. Chaerephon slipped back between the rocks as the snow began to fall harder and pressed his skinny arms around himself.

Tense silence reigned in the camp as the snow fell harder and faster. Smoke from the sacrifice disappeared into the frigid wind. The minutes ticked by slowly.

Chaerephon kept his eyes on the enemy below until the snow fell too thick to see them any longer. Perhaps this was the miracle they had prayed for.

Morning came, and no sign of the Tyrants and their army was left on hillside. The enemy had become disoriented in the snow and been forced to turn around. Their prayers had been answered.

403 BCE, Athens

Socrates received a summons from a messenger of the Tyrants.

"Your presence has been requested to go fetch the general Leon from Salamis to be put to death for his crimes," the young man said to Socrates.

Socrates shook his head. Leon was a democrat whose only crime was not supporting the politics of the Thirty Tyrants. Executing this man in cold blood was not something that Socrates could do and maintain the consistency of character and justice that he had spent many years seeking after.

"I won't go," he told the messenger.

The messenger hesitated, looking around him at the men hurriedly taking care of business in the Agora around them. He looked afraid of Socrates' refusal, as if it would cause the Tyrants to take his life along with Socrates'.

Socrates understood that in order to gain more of a foothold within the community, the Tyrants felt that they needed to implicate as many Athenians as they could in their evil, Socrates included.

"I don't care at all about death," Socrates said. "I want no part of this scheme. You can tell them that."

When it became clear that Socrates was not going to change his mind on the matter, the messenger ducked his head and walked quickly in the direction from which he had come.

Socrates knew that he would be named as an enemy of the State for his refusal. He was not wrong. But before Critias could send a mob after him and erase his life from history for all time, the democrats from windblown Phyle came down from their haven and through the Piraeus to meet the Thirty Tyrants in a battle that would bring them a step closer to regaining their city.

Critias and another of the Thirty, Charmides, were killed in the battle, and the rest of the Thirty withdrew back into Athens to figure out their next move. The Athenians, however, would not hear of it. The 3,000 citizens left in the city removed the oligarchy from power and elected new representatives.

The Spartans sent in diplomats to attempt to bring Athens back under its thumb. Democrats who had lived the last year in exile flooded back into the city to reclaim their places in society. Among them was the bitter democrat, Anytus.

While Sparta didn't succeed in squelching the democrats once again, the effects of its temporary takeover reverberated amongst the Athenians for years to come.

CHAPTER FIVE: SOCRATES' CONVICTION

399 BCE, Athens

Socrates stood before the five hundred members of the jury, his friends, and the curious onlookers from all over Athens and surrounding territories. All of these men had been made rough from the hardship they had survived under the Thirty Tyrants. Many of them had had to kill fellow Athenians in order to survive and carry out horrific acts by the orders of a tyrannical oligarchy.

While many of them had originally found Socrates to be an interesting character to wander about the Agora talking with at one time, they were now offended by his optimism as well as his lack of involvement in political life, and his propensity for turning all they held dear—success, wealth, military and political prowess—into frivolity before their very eyes. His unmoving opinions, at first endearing years ago, now infuriated them.

The naïve-sounding questions that he had asked in his youth had been endearing; in his old age, these questions were tactless and offensive. How dare he question their morality when they'd each done what they'd had to do to survive?

"No matter what verdict is found today, I won't stop in my questioning, for I am charged by God and have a duty to the people of Athens, to all of you, to persuade you to take care of your souls," Socrates said. "Wealth doesn't bring virtue, but virtue, by its nature, can bring wealth, a good reputation, and all good things. This is my philosophy, and if this is what is corrupting the youth, then perhaps I am a bad person.

"Acquit me or condemn me, but it doesn't matter. I won't stop in my mission to bring virtue to the forefront of my city even if I am killed a million times."

The crowd, unable to keep silent at this, burst forth with anger. Raucous booing echoed off the stone walls and pillars. A few cheers mingled with the jeers, but they could not overcome them.

"Men of Athens," he called out over the noise. "Do not interrupt me."

The rabble calmed down with great reluctance.

"If you condemn me, you will be doing a disservice to your community, for God has called me to give the gift of honesty to you all. You need me. It won't be easy to find someone else like me, and so I urge you not to take my life, to spare me."

He recounted the time he was called by the Thirty Tyrants to bring Leon of Salamis to be executed and take his money. He had refused at great risk to his life. "I refused to do that which I knew was wrong, not caring one bit about my own death."

He also recounted another incident in which he had been called upon as an official to vote to illegally execute eight disgraced Athenian generals who had negligently lost the lives of 4,000 of their men. Though he stood firm in his desire to acquit them, as was the law, his solitary vote was overruled, and the six who were in Athens were killed immediately.

"If any adults here were corrupted by me in their youth," Socrates said, "I ask that you please come forward and accuse me to my face."

He gazed into the pool of familiar faces. "Crito?" he asked.

Crito shook his head.

"Plato?"

Plato also shook his head.

Socrates went down the list of followers who were present there in the room, and each in turn denied having been corrupted by him. "I ask you now, Meletus, to go out and find the former pupils of mine who you claim that I've corrupted and get them to verify your claim against me. They must exist if you say so."

Meletus smirked. "I will do no such thing," he said. "But I think we all remember Alcibiades, who turned to drunkenness and depravity."

Many in the crowd nodded, remembering the charming, beautiful, golden haired man who drove men and women alike to lustful distraction. He had no self-control when it came to drink and sex. His wife had tried to divorce him for bringing home prostitutes to sleep with all the time, and he'd dragged her back to his house in a selfish, drunken haze.

Meletus continued. "And who could hope to forget the dreadful tyranny of your students, Critias and Charmides, who caused such vicious violence to us all while you made their list of acceptable citizens."

The audience and jurors grumbled their agreement. None of them would live to forget Critias and his reign of terror that had turned them all into beasts for a twelve month span of time.

"My dear Athenians," Socrates said. "I have previously pointed out that I never took money for my teaching. You have heard today the virtuous code by which I have chosen to live my life and all the opportunities I had to act in opposition to it and yet remained steadfast. Am I to be responsible if those with whom I took meals chose not to heed my most ardent teachings?"

As Socrates drew his defense to a close, he left his audience with the following words, "To you and to God I commit my cause, and I hope that your verdict will be one that is beneficial to you as well as to me."

Socrates fell silent.

A rustle in the crowd produced a couple of Socrates' friends, carrying a chair to the front of the room for the elderly man to sit on.

The five hundred jury members filed out of the room. The silence was followed by the roar of the crowd. Everyone in the room spoke to each other at once, speculating about what the jury would vote for.

Socrates' friends rushed to his side.

"They will find you innocent," one of his friends optimistically declared. Some others offered their agreement, telling him that his defense had been flawless.

Socrates looked at them fondly. "They will find me guilty," he said. "But perhaps it is a small price to pay for the good of my beloved Athens."

The jury was out for a little over an hour. The process was a fairly simple one. Each of the five hundred members was given two bronze tokens in the shape of a disk. One token had a hole punched through it, and that token meant a vote of "guilty." The other token was left in tact and meant a vote of "not guilty." Every man made his choice and tossed the corresponding token into a box or a basket.

The four jury members chosen by lot before the votes took place dumped the basket of tokens out and counted them methodically in order to reach the verdict.

The first half of the trial was complete. The jury filed back into the hall.

A weathered old man was chosen by lot to read the verdict and stepped to the front of the hall. The crowd waited, its cumulative breath held in anticipation of this moment. If the verdict was innocent, Socrates would be free to go about his business.

"The jury has voted," the man said. "By a vote of 280 to 220, Socrates of Alopeke has been found guilty."

The crowds rumbled, many with relief for having chosen the winning side, and a surprising number of them with chagrin.

As was the typical procedure, Socrates was allowed to stand once again and petition the jury for his punishment. This was when most defendants begged for mercy and proposed a penalty to replace capital punishment. Perhaps, even still, it was not too late for Socrates to play on the jury's heartstrings to extract a more lenient punishment.

Socrates, however, had no such idea in mind. He stood from his chair at the front of the room and cleared his throat with confidence. The expression that graced his features was equal parts defiance and pride.

"Men of Athens, I am saddened by your choice to condemn me," he said. "It is as I had expected. But I am surprised that the vote was so close. If thirty of you had voted differently, I would be a free man. Now you ask me what a fitting punishment would be for a poor man who has only helped the State of Athens.

"You expect me to name the punishment I deserve, and yet I have done nothing to harm anyone. You expect me to name a penalty that might replace the penalty of death. I could sentence myself to prison, but then I will be a slave to the State and its officials. I could name a fine, but I am too poor to pay it and would only end up in prison. I could go into exile, but if my own countrymen can't stand me, then what chance have I anywhere else? I will not cease my questions, so the same this is likely to happen again.

"I am not sure if accepting death for all the crimes I haven't committed is good or evil. To name a penalty when I have committed no crime is certainly evil, and I refuse to do it, just because Meletus threatens me.

"I will, however, offer an alternative to my death. I will pay a fine of one mina. Since I am poor and don't have even that small sum, I will borrow it from my friends." Socrates looked over at his friends. Plato, Crito, Critobulus, Apollodorus, and the others had raised thirty minae, fearing that the jury would ask for far more than one mina. "In fact," he said, "they have loaned me thirty minae, and that is the amount which I am prepared to offer. My friends' good characters are your proof that they will pay the full amount."

With that, the jury retired once again to cast a vote.

The first vote may have been closer than expected, but Socrates' blatant mockery of the Athenian legal system in proposing a fine as small as one mina swayed many who had originally been on his side. Perhaps if he'd admitted his guilt, begged for mercy, and proposed the fine of thirty minae at the outset, the jury might have spared his life. It was still not a large sum but a large enough sum for a poor old man with nothing and a large enough sum to indicate that Socrates had taken the trial seriously.

The final vote came in at 360 to 140 in favor of the death penalty.

CHAPTER SIX: THE DEATH OF SOCRATES

Before Dawn, May, 399 BCE, Athens

A few rays of sun simmered on the eastern horizon, not yet piercing the fog that hung over Athens. The sacred ship, which was sent every year to Delos, was in the harbor, a sign that the State was now allowed to perform its executions. Many years ago, a monster that was half man, half bull had lived on Crete, and a group of children was put on a ship and sailed to it every year to be offered as a sacrifice to it.

The barbaric practice halted only when the hero, Theseus, went to the island himself and killed the monster. In celebration, every year a sacred ship was sent to the temple of Apollo on the island of Delos. No executions were to be performed while the holy delegation was away.

Socrates had thus been chained within the prison for nearly a month waiting for the day of his execution.

Socrates sat chained in his prison cell, having awakened to Plato standing next to his cell looking in on him morosely.

"How long have you stood there?" Socrates asked.

"Won't you please consider fleeing?" Plato said. "I have a large sum in my bag, and I can pay your guards off. The others would gladly steal you away to Phyle or someplace else where you can hide until things blow over."

"I won't run and put myself into exile," Socrates said. "We've already discussed this. I said the same thing to Crito two mornings ago."

They had, and he had. Socrates refused to run away from his execution like a criminal fleeing out of guilt. Death could be no worse than living as an exile from his beloved city of Athens.

"What of Xanthippe and your sons?" Plato said. "Your youngest is still a baby. You won't want to leave them orphaned, surely." In Athens, children were considered to be orphans when their father died, even if their mother was still living.

"Xanthippe has never needed me, and if she does, I have many friends who will be glad to help her out," Socrates said. He looked significantly at Plato.

"Of course. I will do everything in my power, but...you won't reconsider?"

"I will not. I have spent my whole life in service to Athens, and I will not in my last moments nullify all that I have spoken."

"As you wish," Plato said. He stared at the ground for a long moment. When he looked up and met Socrates eyes, he took a breath and leaned forward as if to try one more argument. Then, sensing that it would do no good, he shook his head slightly and looked back at the ground. "I will miss you."

"Take care that you never forget yourself," Socrates said to the younger man.

Plato nodded, still not meeting Socrates' eyes.

"Remember, son. The unexamined life is not worth living."

Shortly after Plato had left, the Eleven came in to prepare him for his last day of life.

The pestle ground against the mortar, stone on stone, crushing the hemlock leaves along with the poppy seeds that would ease some of the symptoms that went along with the poison—muscle spasms, cramps, convulsions.

Socrates' friends gathered with him for his last moments in this world. He had sent away Xanthippe and their small son, Menexenos. Like a good Athenian wife, Xanthippe had seen to her husband's care while he was in prison, feeding and watering him and making plans for slaves to clean out his cell once he'd vacated it. Many families of prisoners left them in the cell alone without food or water, and they perished before their execution.

Xanthippe had shown up the morning of the execution to wail, shake her fists at the gods in heaven, beat her forehead, and scrape at her face with her nails. Socrates sent her away, perhaps thinking her unworthy to participate in his last moments on earth or perhaps wanting to spare her the horrors of witnessing her husband's slow death. He would have an untraditional death.

He even went to the effort to bathe himself in the prison's cistern so that no one would have to do it for him after he was dead.

He watched his friends enter the prison to see him.

Plato was noticeably absent. Socrates was disappointed not to see him but not surprised. Matters of life and death were always more difficult to bear for a young man than they were for an old man.

It was customary for the convicted to put off his execution until late in the day, and those gathered around him began a discussion. First they spoke of Aesop's Fables, which Socrates had been reading.

"I heard that you're trying your hand at writing poetry about the fables," the poet, Evenus said.

"I have no intention of being your competition," Socrates said. "Not that such a thing would be an easy task. I simply had a dream that I should try composing music, and what is music but poetry? I tried turning a few stories into verses."

The talk soon turned to more serious things, like the nature of the soul and body. Was the soul mortal? Did it dissipate with the death of the body? Socrates felt that the soul resembled the divine and would go on existing even when the mortal body had been snuffed out.

"The invisible soul," Socrates said, "must leave the visible body for the invisible world, that is, the divine, immortal, rational world which is free from the foolishness and mistakes of men with their irrational fears and passions, and stay forever in the presence of the gods."

When he could put off his death no longer, he excused himself to bathe and to see his wife and children for the last time ever. Clean and cold, he returned to his friends in his prison cell.

The jailor came into the cell, trembling with fear and dread. He had come to know and admire Socrates during the month of his imprisonment.

"Forgive me for what the State is making me do to you," the man said. "Please don't blame me. I don't want to do this." He looked imploringly into Socrates' eyes, but before Socrates could answer, the guard's eyes filled with tears, and he fled from the room wailing.

The jailor's attendants came a minute later, bringing Socrates the fateful cup. He picked up the cup that contained the fatal dose of hemlock poison.

"What should I do after I drink it?" Socrates asked. The State always preferred for the convicted to administer the poison himself. The Greeks could be squeamish when it came to the death penalty. Violent deaths were not preferred by the State.

"You will only have to walk around until your legs get heavy. Then you may lie down, and the poison will do its job."

He raised the cup to his lips, looking around at his friends, who held their breath in fearful anticipation. Perhaps some of them wished that Socrates would turn into a coward at the last second and refuse to drink.

Not a hint of fear or cowardice showed on his face as he drank the liquid in one swallow. The dill improved the flavor, but the shot of poison tasted deadly all the same.

His friends, seeing the poison gone from the cup, couldn't keep their sorrow from welling up in them. Many of them cried out. Tears wet their cheeks and fell on the dirty floor.

"What are you doing?" Socrates asked. "I sent the women away in order to avoid all of this crying. Don't you think a man should die in peace? Have patience. I will be gone soon enough, and then you can all wail like women."

The young men, with great effort, got control of their emotions for the sake of their teacher. Two of them walked with him on either side around the prison cell, as he'd been directed by the jail attendants. When his legs became too heavy to lift, they helped him to lie down on his back.

Socrates' death was a State-sponsored suicide, and it was a lot less messy than most other forms of execution that the Greeks could employ. In some cases, a poison would cause convulsing and blood, but in the case of hemlock, the poison numbed the extremities before the poison reached the brain. By the time it hit the brain, convulsions might have happened except that the limbs were now immobile. He was lucky to be going in such a manner.

He stroked Phaedo's soft hair. "Tomorrow you may cut your beautiful hair off," he said. Then he pulled a covering over his face. Death, despite everyone around one at its moment, was still a private experience, he felt.

The attendant tapped Socrates' foot. "Do you feel that?" he asked.

"I do not," Socrates said.

A few minutes later, the attendant tapped his leg higher up. "Do you feel that?"

"No."

The poison was gradually working its way up. When it reached his heart, he would be gone.

A few minutes passed in silence. The attendant tapped him again, and he didn't flinch.

He struggled to move his hand to remove the covering, all of a sudden needing to say one last thing. "Crito, we owe a cock to Asclepius. Don't forget to pay him my debt."

"Of course," Crito said. "Is there anything else that you need me to do for you?"

Socrates didn't answer. His face was frozen. No air passed over his lips.

Crito reached his hand out and carefully closed Socrates' eyes and mouth. Around him, weeping echoed off the stone prison walls like a soft rain.

CHAPTER SEVEN: PLATO'S DISILLUSIONMENT

June, 399 BCE, Athens

Plato, son of Ariston and Perictione, a descendent of Athenian and Messenian kings, and a relative of the statesman Solon, made his way south through evening sun in the Agora. The sun didn't fit his mood. It should be raining. Why didn't Zeus strike all of Athens down with thunder? That would be much more fitting.

He carried a rooster under his arm. In their grief, they'd forgotten about the rooster Socrates had requested that they sacrifice on his behalf, but it was better a couple of days late than not at all.

The sanctuary of Asclepius was relatively new to the Athenian acropolis, having been erected about twenty years ago. Asclepius was popular with the Spartans, the sworn enemies to the city of Athena. He was a god of healing, and the sanctuary had been erected while Athens had been licking the wounds of plague and starvation.

What exactly had Socrates meant by the sacrifice? Had he meant to ask Asclepius to cure him from the poison? Plato didn't think so. Perhaps he'd meant that death was the only cure for his life. Perhaps he'd meant to get in one final jab at those who had sentenced him to death. The Athenian people openly worshipped the god of their enemies even while they accused Socrates of worshipping a different god. Did he mean that he believed that Asclpius would bring him back to life? No amount of puzzling was bringing Plato closer to what Socrates had intended it to mean.

He leaned over slightly as he began to climb the acropolis hill. The sanctuary of Asclepius came into view. The white marble shone in the sun like a cloud in the sky. He walked the last few paces, noting that the sun was at the perfect spot, just above the horizon. It was time to make the sacrifice.

Inside the sanctuary, Plato killed the rooster and knelt to pray. His eyes drifted closed. He felt as though he hadn't slept in a long time. He rested there on the floor at the feet of Asclepius, letting his heart be the voice that his body was too weary to summon.

The room grew dark. He felt himself drifting away.

A rooster crowed in the distance. Plato awoke. Light filtered through the entry of the sanctuary. He tried to get to his feet from his crouched position, but his legs had gone numb. He leaned to the side and pulled his legs out from under his body. He let the lifeblood prick his legs and bring life back into them.

Again, a rooster crowed somewhere in the distance. One rooster had been sacrificed, but a new rooster was crowing. Socrates might be dead, but Plato was alive, and so were his friends.

All at once, he had an idea. He would record the life and death of Socrates himself, using his own memories of the great, wise man as well as the memories of his other friends. He would write the story of the trial and of the unjust way in which he died. He would make it so that even though Socrates was dead, he wouldn't be able to stay dead. Athens would realize the mistake it had made.

He thought about the decision he'd been laboring over for the past several months, which was whether to have a political career. It was the logical thing for a man of his connections to do, and he might do some good for the State, but the idea of participating in a government that had condemned his friend to death soured his stomach. His decision was made. It was like Socrates had said—a politician could not remain just and good for very long.

Someone entered the sanctuary. "Hey," the stranger said. "Aren't you a follower of Socrates, the man who was killed for impiety?"

Plato stood. "I was just leaving," he said, and he left the sanctuary without looking back. Perhaps it was time that he left Athens for a bit and did some traveling. He needed to go someplace where he wouldn't feel as if he needed to look over his shoulder to watch his back everywhere he went.

July, 398 BCE, Megara

Plato walked the perimeter of the gymnasium. He'd been in Megara for almost a year now, having come here with a number of Socrates' supporters who had also needed to get away from Athens for a while.

Watching the young men train for the Isthmian games was bringing back memories of his own youth, not so terribly long ago. He'd been a champion wrestler. He wondered if any of these young men had heard of him. A few of them glanced at him as he took a spot on the sidelines in front of the bleachers to watch. A couple of the trainers looked at him suspiciously, as if he might be a foreign trainer come to scope out the competition right before the big event.

Plato's eyes were drawn to one young man in particular. He was well formed and beautiful. A sheen of sweat covered his skin, and his trainer barked orders at him like a military general. The young man had put his competitor in a headlock, but it was clear by the quivering of his muscles that he was barely in control of the opponent. Plato wondered how long he'd been scrimmaging today.

The sun was beginning its descent toward the western horizon. Many of the competitors had already stopped their training for the day.

"Stop," the trainer barked.

The young athlete released his opponent.

"That was sloppy. You executed that move perfectly this morning. What's wrong with you? You need to focus."

The young man's jaw tensed. He was tired but unwilling to admit as much. Plato recognized the set of that jaw. He wanted to win, and he was convinced that his trainer knew best.

The trainer was a retired war general with a reputation as one of the fiercest warriors on the battlefield and in the wrestling ring. His athletes took the crown every year. Competition for his services was fierce, and if one competitor failed to live up to his expectations, he could find another one with no effort.

Plato shook his head. He'd learned the hard way that there was such a thing as too much training. Before the trainer could command the man to try again, Plato strode toward them.

"You need to rest," he said.

The trainer turned a fierce gaze on him. "What gives you the authority to contradict me?"

Plato introduced himself and let the introduction sink in for a moment. The trainer had heard of him. Then he continued. "Temperance in all things is good, but in sports, it is absolutely essential. Let me tell you why."

August, 411 BCE, Delphi

On the hot, bright morning that the Pythian games were to start, Plato woke up early to stretch and warm up his muscles. Since he'd taken the victory a year ago at the Isthmian games, he'd trained even harder than ever in order to win the victorious laurel wreath of the god Apollo.

But it wasn't just the crown that he'd gain. With it, he would have all the glory and fame of winning along with a shot at being chosen to represent Athens in the Olympic games. The winner of the Olympics would receive a far greater reward than a laurel wreath—he would receive free meals for the rest of his life. Last year, winning the Isthmian games had won him a bottle of olive oil that was too large for a man to carry. He'd divided the oil into smaller containers and sold most of them at a high price.

Yesterday he'd performed his hardest workout yet, and he'd felt strong and ready. Today should be a cinch. He stood, and his muscles immediately protested. Perhaps this was his punishment for sneaking away from the festivities early yesterday in order to train.

According to legend, mother earth had accidentally created a giant, deadly python during the creation of the world. The python roamed the earth terrorizing humans until Apollo decided to hunt it and kill it. Shooting almost every arrow from his quiver, he eventually struck down the python in victory. So that no one would forget his heroic deed, he created the Pythian games and set up the temple for the oracle of Delphi in honor of his triumph.

This legend was reenacted in a drama. There was a procession and a festival sacrifice that was performed in the Temple of Apollo.

Men and women from all over Greece came to celebrate. A truce to all wars was called; the point of these games and festivities wasn't political but religious, and all those who worshipped Apollo were invited to the most important religious site in the world. After four days of these festivities, the games finally began.

Plato became increasingly nervous when his tired muscles didn't lose their soreness. As the morning continued, he hoped against hope that it wouldn't hurt his shot at the wreath. His competitors greeted him, their smiles fierce and competitive. Plato shared their smile, masking his uncertainty. Many of them recognized him from his victory last summer. He was a top contender in the wrestling category.

He took his place at the ready for his first match. His opponent was strong, but Plato was more clever and took him down easily. The second match was more difficult, as the man was larger. Plato might have been stronger than him had his muscles not been so sore from yesterday. It was only with a complicated series of side steps and a surprise lunge that he was able to beat him.

His coach, a man by the name of Ariston of Argos, noticed his lack of strength. "You haven't won by much. Why aren't you strong today?" he asked.

Plato frowned, not wanting to tell him why the gods were punishing him. Ariston had told him that too much exercise before a match would make him weaker instead of stronger, but Plato had doubted him, because it had seemed illogical. Perhaps Ariston just hadn't wanted to miss any of the festivities and was making excuses.

"You snuck away yesterday," Ariston said. "Did you go to the gymnasium as I told you not to?"

Plato hung his head further.

"Now you know why I said not to. You have likely cost yourself the crown."

And that had been the case. His final match should have been his. The opponent was quick and strong, but not more so than Plato. But Plato's body was nearly shaking with exhaustion from the series of matches he'd already fought. He gave it his all, but in the end, he was pinned to the ground and unable to arise.

July, 398 BCE, Megara

"I took second place," Plato said to the trainer and the young competitor. "But as you know, there is no prize for coming in second. That is why it is important to practice temperance. Fatigue to your muscles isn't your friend this close to the Games."

The coach looked at Plato stonily, but grudgingly turned his gaze to his pupil and commanded him to rest for the next few days.

Years later, Plato would go on to teach his students to master a balance between physical and mental training at his Academy, saying that one who only exercises his body develops a certain type of mind and one who only exercise his mind develops a certain type of body. The former will be excessively uncivilized in thought, and the latter will be indecently soft in body.

CHAPTER EIGHT: PLATO AND THE FALL OF ATHENS

405 BCE, Aegospotami *

The small river called Aegospotami flowed between the gently sloping hills that gave way to the Hellespont just to the northeast of Sestos. Nearby, a meteor had fallen out of the sky about sixty years previously leaving a crater the size of a wagon. Astrologers noted that at the same time, a comet now known as Halley's Comet had appeared in the night sky.

---

* It's improbable that Plato actually fought in this battle. Since historians agree that Plato was of age at the time of the war, and that most men who were of age during the Peloponnesian War fought during its course, it can be extrapolated that Plato was likely to have fought at some point, though no primary sources exist that confirm this. I have chosen to put Plato into this particular battle, because it is the definitive battle of the war and, as thus, would have played heavily into Plato's experience and Athenian worldview at the time.

Astronomical anomalies aside, however, Aegospotami was the location of the decisive battle between Athens and Sparta in the Peloponnesian War.

The Athenians were coming off of a surprising victory at the Battle of Arginusae. Their fleets and men had been decidedly less trained and less experienced than the Peloponnesian fleet and soldiers, and yet they managed to pull out a win for the team. The casualties were so great for both sides, however, that winning at Arginusae was not the pivotal victory that Athens was pulling for.

After this, the Spartans once again put Lysander in command of the Spartan navy. Though the Spartan law forbade a commander from taking the office of the *navarch* multiple times, Lysander was again given the role along with the title of vice admiral.

Lysander was the best decision Sparta could have made. Because of his connection with Prince Cyrus of Persia, he was able to rapidly rebuild the Spartan fleet. When Prince Cyrus made him the satrap of Asia Minor, Lysander suddenly had all the money and resources he needed for a successful campaign against Athens at his disposal. He sailed through the Aegean Sea taking one Athenian-held city after another until he had established a base in Lampsacus and effectively cut off the trade route of Athens' primary grain supply.

It was time for the Athenians to act if they didn't want Athena's city and her inhabitants to all slowly starve to death.

The Athenian fleet sped to Sestos, where they set up their own base. Then, they marched over the hills to Aegospotami, where they could set up camp much closer to Lysander and his troops at Lampsacus. The idea was that they wanted to be able to keep a close eye on Lysander's every move.

What the Athenians forgot to think hard enough about was the inopportune position they had put themselves in by having to maintain a supply line that went all the way to Sestos with no harbor they could sail into to dock near their beach camp.

Plato was a member of the cavalry, as was fitting for a man of his family lineage and connections. Horses were rare and expensive, and only a wealthy man could afford to buy one and maintain it.

As the troops set up camp along the beach, Plato scouted the area on horseback making sure that the area didn't house any unwanted enemy guests. In the distance, he saw a lone rider traversing the beach area. He pushed his horse to a run and overtook the rider.

The rider slowed, allowing Plato to catch up with him. Plato's hand tensed over his spear just in case. No sooner had he formed a plan in his mind in case the rider attacked than he recognized who the soldier was. It was Alcibiades, the exiled Athenian general.

"I mean no trouble," Alcibiades said. "I have come to offer some advice." The golden hair that peaked from beneath his helmet shone in the morning sun.

"Let me take you to Philocles. He is the general," Plato said, and the two rode into camp.

Philocles came to greet Alcibiades coolly. "What can I do for you?" he asked.

"I have some advice for you," said Alcibiades. "I don't think this is a wise place to make camp. I'd send the fleet back to Sestos. It will be more secure there and will be closer to your supplies."

"This is the best way for us to keep an eye on Lysander," Philocles said. "He is bound to come this way to attack us, and we will be ready for him here."

"Forgive me if I disagree with you."

"You may disagree, but you are not in charge," Philocles said. "My plan is to send my fleet to where Lysander's is docked in the harbor at Lampsacus and await them at the entrance. There will be nowhere for him to go."

"Perhaps I should have been in charge," Alcibiades said. "I've never heard of you, but I am clearly more experienced than you are. This plan won't work. I have a proposition for you."

Philocles' expression turned dark. He was a proud man and didn't want to share a victory with Athens' greatest playboy, but he must have seen the weakness in his own plan, because he stared at Alcibiades until he continued to speak rather than cutting him off.

"There are a number of Thracian kings who have offered to lend me an army," Alcibiades said. "If you will share the command with me, I can help you chase Lysander away from Lampsacus."

Philocles called the other Athenian generals over, and Alcibiades related the same information to them that he'd told Philocles. The generals withdrew up the riverbank to discuss the matter, leaving Alcibiades and Plato next to their horses staring out over the waves.

Like every man in Athens, Plato had heard all of the outrageous gossip surrounding Alcibiades, Athena's golden child. He had once entered seven chariots in the Olympic chariot races and had three of them come in at the top of the heap—first, second, and fourth.

People said that he liked to saunter about the city in a deep purple cloak, the color of aristocracy. Some said he liked that it looked like congealed blood. Some said that he was an enemy of democracy. Others said that he was merely an attention-seeking young man who behaved foolishly. In any case, he certainly had a reputation for always taking things one step past the line of reason.

Socrates had made some mentions of the man—how he would come to dinner and get more wildly drunk than any man in the room before the meal was even over and then have sex with any man, woman, or slave he chose. Sometimes, he went out after these symposiums to brothels to sleep with prostitutes, sometimes male and sometimes female.

It was said that the man's loyalties were difficult to pin down and that he was as likely as not to change his side on a whim. Plato wasn't a fan of the pretty man. It seemed clear that the man's beauty had been wasted. It was a pity. Yet, Plato also recognized that Alcibiades possessed a much more likely plan of attack than the current Athenian generals. They'd heard rumors about Lysander's liaison with Persia. If Lysander had the Persian army at his disposal, then Athens couldn't win. The soldiers and commanders for Athens were amateurs, inexperienced at battle and at fighting. Many of them had died at Arginusae, and there weren't enough replacements to refresh them for the next move.

The generals crossed back over to Alcibiades. Philocles shook his head. "We will continue according to plan."

Alcibiades stared at him for a long moment. Then, he swung up on his horse. "Your loss," he said and kicked his horse into action. He sped back up the beach and disappeared over the hill, where his castle sat hugged between two hills.

A few mornings later, the fleet disembarked to Lampsacus to meet Lysander's fleet in its harbor. They waited outside for most of the day, and Lysander didn't meet them for a battle.

Philocles and the generals made the assumption that he wasn't going to fight today and returned to their beach. The soldiers got off the ship and scattered across the beach to scrounge for food and fuel for the campfires that the drizzle had put out while they were gone.

A few hours later, a crack split the air louder than thunder. Plato rode to the top of the hill he was mounting in time to see the enemy fleet bearing down hard on the unprotected Athenian ships. The first ship was smashed by the hull of one of Lysander's much larger ships. A second ship caught on fire.

Plato sent up the alarm.

The enemy was already making its way to shore in smaller paddleboats. The few Athenian soldiers who were lounging at the camp picked up their weapons and ran to beat the Spartans off, but many of them weren't wearing their bulky, uncomfortable armor and were run through almost immediately.

Plato wondered fleetingly what kind of liberty this war was. It had tied up twenty years of resources and depleted Athens' population gruesomely. Many men were obligated to take two wives as a pragmatic solution for population growth. Many didn't even want one wife. A wife was generally considered to be one of those necessary evils of society. You couldn't live with them, and you couldn't live without them.

Now, the only outcome this battle could possibly have was a great loss to Athens. Plato watched as a few of the Athenian ships turned away from the beach and headed out to sea. They wouldn't make it far. He watched as first one and then another had their hulls broken by the enemy ships. He could imagine the Spartans jumping aboard, fighting the Athenians hand-to-hand, and jumping back to their own ships just in time to watch the Athenians sink.

I should go down and fight, Plato thought. He didn't want to. He could ride away now, and no one would notice that he was missing. After all, he could easily claim to have been on his way to Sestos for supplies.

Hoof beats pounded the ground. "What's going on?" a man asked. A couple of riders slowed up next to Plato.

"Battle," he said. Then, he kicked his horse to action. He wouldn't be caught in cowardice or disloyalty. He ran through several Spartans and was able to quickly retreat from spears aimed his way, because he was on a horse, but it wasn't enough.

He heard one of the generals give the retreat command, and everyone on the beach who was alive fled as quickly as they could. Plato grabbed a fellow soldier running alongside him.

"Put your foot in the stirrup," he yelled at the man. The man put his foot up, stumbling as the horse pulled him faster than he could keep up. Plato pulled the man by the wrist, swinging him onto the horse behind him.

Later, they learned that very few men had survived the surprise attack. The nine ships that had attempted escape had been captured or sunk. It was a glowing victory for Sparta and a desolate loss for Athens.

CHAPTER NINE: PLATO'S PERSONAL STRUGGLE WITH ATHENS

397 BCE, Megara

Plato was becoming restless with his stay at Euclid's home in Megara. He was grateful, but it was time to move on. He wasn't ready to return to Athens, but there was a wide world out there to explore. Perhaps he should check out Egypt.

Euclid entered the yard where Plato stood staring into the distance. He was a slight, quiet man. Looking at him, one expected him to be a very reserved, conservative man whose most adventurous accomplishment was coaxing a merchant into giving him a bargain at the market. One would have been wrong.

When Socrates had been alive, Euclid had loved coming into Athens to hear him lecture and teach. Unfortunately, Athens started banning Megaran citizens from entering the city. Not to be deterred, Euclid disguised himself as a woman and snuck inside the walls under the cloak of night when the women were out about their business in Athens. Then he'd sneak around the city until he heard Socrates' voice, throw off his disguise, and sit down with whichever young men were there at the time.

Euclid had been present at Socrates' execution and had offered several of his followers refuge in his home in Megara afterward.

"I'm going to start a school," Euclid said.

"Here in Megara?" Plato asked.

Euclid nodded. "Are you interested in teaching?"

Plato thought for a moment, though he knew what his answer would be. Euclid was a good man and wise in many ways. Like Socrates had taught, Euclid believed that the greatest knowledge was to understand goodness. Unlike Socrates, he believed in a more Eleatic line of reasoning—that the greatest knowledge was knowledge of one universal being, which was the goodness. This wouldn't have been such a great point of contention, but Plato didn't follow Euclid's method of proving his ideas at all. Euclid would take someone else's conclusion, ignore the premises it was based on, and disprove it by drawing absurd consequences. He rarely directly explained why his idea was right, instead preferring to explain why the other was wrong.

"I know we think differently on some matters," Euclid said, "but perhaps your mind will provide a balance to mine and give students a more well-rounded perspective."

"You've thought this through?" Plato asked.

"For quite a while," Euclid said.

"I can't stay here," Plato said.

Euclid sighed. "I know. But it was worth the ask."

"Interesting idea, though, starting a school."

"Perhaps you can start one in Athens once things calm down a little," Euclid said.

Plato nodded. The seed rooted itself in his mind. Perhaps he would do exactly that. "I'm going to go to Egypt," he said.

March, 404 BCE, Athens

All of Athens' fleet had been lost to Lysander at Aegospotami. Not only did they have no fleet with which to wage war against the Spartan general but, more importantly, they had no way to ship food from across the Black Sea into Athens. Lysander's siege would soon end, and it wasn't likely to be pretty for the Athenians who were starving and dying of disease.

Plato laid low, sometimes with Socrates and several of his followers and sometimes with his relatives. His mother and stepfather's connections meant that he did not starve as the poor and unconnected did, though he wondered at the justice of it all.

It was said that none of the generals, Philocles included, had been spared. Plato wondered not for the first time if things would have been different if Philocles had humbled himself and taken Alcibiades' help.

A knock sounded at the door. Plato stood to open it, and Critias and Charmides entered.

"Athens has surrendered at last," Critias said. He pompously flipped his wavy hair from his forehead.

"I heard," Plato said, assuming that it was pointless for him to point out that everyone in Athens already knew this bit of information. The wall had been bashed in days ago, and food had been brought through and distributed messily in the Agora with one man pushing another man to the ground to grab it before it disappeared.

"I have been put in charge of establishing the Spartan rule in Athens," Critias said. "They are willing to spare us but not our democracy, which I personally don't think is such a bad thing. They liked my ideas for rehabilitating the city." His eyes glinted coldly.

Plato could only imagine what Critias had in mind.

"There's a place for you in the new government if you want it," he said.

Plato did a double take. That wasn't what he'd expected. He had been talking a lot about virtue and government with Socrates. Perhaps this was his opportunity to promote the ideals of justice and goodness in a community that was broken from so much hardship.

"What are your ideas for rehabilitating Athens?" Plato asked.

"First things first, we need to get rid of everyone who might be a threat to the new government. No sense letting a civil war happen under our noses. Then, we've got to raise money. I'm thinking we might as well combine them. We eliminate the threats and confiscate their wealth and property in the same move. I've started a list."

"That will cost you much more than it will gain you," Plato said.

"I don't see how."

Plato sighed. He'd listened to the debate between Thrasymachus and Socrates not too long ago regarding just and unjust rulers. A just person will want to outdo an unjust person but not a just person. An unjust person will want to outdo everyone. As such, wouldn't the just band together against the unjust, since they don't care about outdoing each other, while the unjust ban together with no one, because they must try to outdo everyone?

But Plato, remembering the way he'd witnessed neighbor fighting neighbor over a loaf of bread, recalled how the conversation had continued. Injustice causes hatred, which leads to civil war. People committing injustices against each other would learn to hate each other and continue in their injustices. Perhaps all Critias would have to do was feed their hatred of each other, and he and his oligarchy would never have to fear for their own lives.

Plato sighed again. Regardless of the outcome, he wanted no part in the injustice Critias would bring to Athens. "I'm not interested," he said.

"I won't ask you again," Critias said, eyes glinting.

Plato hesitated for the smallest moment. "I won't want you to. Politics and public offices are tempting because they seem to give a man the best chance for success, but I'd rather be a philosopher. The rewards of philosophy are greater, even though they are less apparent immediately."

Critias scoffed, as Plato knew he would. High offices and great wealth had always attracted Critias more than they ought to have.

389 BCE, Egypt

The Egyptians believed that the sun was a symbol of the creator god due to its role in bringing life and light to the earth. They had observed that the moon was unlike the sun in that it failed to produce light or warmth of its own, instead reflecting that of the sun based on its position in the sky in relation to the sun and earth.

Plato had been studying Egyptian cosmology under the tutelage of the Horite priest, Sechnuphis, for many years now. He'd heard that one of the great mathematical thinkers, Pythagoras, had come to Memphis to study in a similar manner and had wanted to do the same.

The Egyptian perspective had afforded him all kinds of new ideas, which he was preparing to compile into a dramatic dialogue that he could use as a teaching tool. In this particular study, he was looking at forms using the allegory of a cave.

In his fictional cave, prisoners were bound facing away from a fire. All statues placed in front of the fire had their shadows projected on the wall in front of them. The shadow that they saw of the statue was a representation of the real statue, and they only had the ability to determine what the real statue was like based on its shadow.

The people in the cave would attribute meanings to the shadows and award prizes to those who could recall facts and orders and repetitions among them, but these prizes would be useless, because the people were not seeing reality.

It wasn't unlike looking at the moon to see what the sun was like.

But what if one of the people in the cave was released from his shackles and allowed to turn around? The light would blind him, but eventually he would learn to see the real statues and believe that they were more real than the shadows. When he turned back to the wall of the cave, he would see that the shadows projected there were not real.

This man would then be taken from the cave and thrust into the daylight. At first, he would be disoriented and look only at the shadows, then at the reflections, and then finally adjust to the reality around him. He would see that the trees and cups and flowers around him were even more real than the statues he had seen in the cave. These things, he realized, must be the most real of all that he had seen. These must be the Forms.

When his eyes fully adjusted to the brightness of the outdoors, the prisoner would finally be able to look up at the sun, which was the source of his being able to see everything around him. The sun was the Form of the Good, and, Plato had come to understand, goodness was the source of understanding.

What, then, was the goal of education? The goal was to drag everyone as far out of the metaphorical cave as possible and point his soul toward the right yearnings.

The problem was that so many people chose to stay in the dark comfort of the cave with their backs to the light, even after a wise man had freed him from his shackles.

The warm, damp air urged a line of sweat down Plato's back as he stared at the night sky, wondering if it was possible to really see accurately. How did he know that the stars he had been gazing at for hours were the true forms or mere reflections of other things, as the moon was? Perhaps he wouldn't ever know, but at least a few things were clearer to him now than they had been before.

It was like Socrates had liked to say: A wise man is one who is willing to admit that he knows nothing.

CHAPTER TEN: PLATO'S FIRST ADVENTURE IN SYRACUSE

387 BCE, Syracuse, Sicily

Dion was the brother-in-law to the ruler of Syracuse, Dionysius I, and the ruler's most trusted advisor. Dion was in charge of managing the embassies that dealt diplomatically with Carthage, one of Syracuse's most persistent enemies, and one that Dionysius I had no patience for dealing with himself. If Carthage was left up to him, he would just as soon break whatever peace treaties he had to in order to knock Carthage off the face of the planet. In fact, he'd already tried this, and when it had backfired, he'd assigned the whole mess to his brother-in-law, who had patched things up rather nicely.

Dion was fantastically wealthy, since Dionysius I, pleased with his advice regarding Carthage, had given him complete access to withdraw money from the Syracusan treasury, so long as he told the tyrant every day when he did so. His house was large by a king's standards and furnished with the best of all the gold and gems that Dionysius I hadn't claimed for himself. Yet, he found that he wasn't happy.

Having been something of an intellectual in his youth, Dion wondered if he should, perhaps, turn his attention back to the acquisition of things that could not be seen.

One day, having heard of the arrival in southern Italy of a philosopher by the name of Plato in the neighboring town of Tarentum, Dion urged Dionysius I to issue the philosopher an invitation to visit him in Syracuse. Dion had heard that Plato had much to say on the subjects of wealth and virtue and wanted to know more.

Plato thought that there was something special about the way the light shone from the sky in the south of Italy. It fell across the ground in such a way that it looked as if the grass might be producing its own light. If Plato had been a poet, he would have been inspired to write great songs about this place. As he stood near the city gate of Tarentum after his walk about the city, a messenger approached him.

"Are you Plato?" the boy asked.

"I am."

"I'm here under the direction of Dionysius I, ruler of Syracuse to invite you to Syracuse to dine with him three days hence."

Plato arrived at the opulent mansion of the tyrant in time for dinner, where the three became acquainted.

"Please stay on for a time and teach me your philosophy," Dion begged.

Plato agreed, seeing in the man a true desire to understand more than mere material things.

Weeks passed. Plato told Dion about his theory of the Forms, and the two talked about the different types of governments and the differences between virtue and vice. Dion got so into their conversations that he started storing away little maxims to use around Dionysius I in hopes of influencing the tyrant positively.

Sayings like, "One of the penalties for refusing to participate in politics is that you end up being governed by your inferiors," and, "There will be no end to the troubles of the states, or of humanity itself, till philosophers become kings in this world, or till those we now call kings and rulers really and truly become philosophers, and political power and philosophy thus come into the same hands," didn't often go over well with the tyrant. Usually, he blew them off, instead asking Dion for the treasury report.

Sometimes he'd snap. "I've been very generous with you," he said. "You've got no cause to criticize me."

"You live in the lap of luxury, and your chief aim of every day is to gain still more gold to store in your tomb," Dion said.

"Last time I checked, your own tomb isn't exactly a poor man's cave."

"Let's have a symposium and invite all of your friends and mine," Dion said. "I already have a menu written. Here." He handed the menu to the testy ruler. "I've exchanged the wine for beer. Plato says that he was a wise man who invented beer. But we can still have wine, too, if that's more preferable to you."

"You mean, you want to invite Plato so that he can preach to me about how un-virtuous I am."

Dion hesitated. "Well, no, not preach. It's a symposium. We'll all discuss things. It will be just like the good old days of Athens. Plato said that they'd all talk very late into the night and then—"

"Fine. Send the invitations. But if anyone starts preaching, I will banish him."

The evening of the symposium arrived. Plato hadn't been sure it was such a great idea when Dion had first brought it up, but Dion had been so excited by the idea of reenacting a night of philosophy akin to those Socrates was invited to in Athens in the so-called glory days, before Lysander had starved the Athenians to their surrender.

The dinner guests, mostly wealthy men of the ruler's acquaintance, arrived and made small talk with each other while they were situated on their couches next to the table. Flute girls played their flutes sweetly around the perimeter of the room. A pitcher of honeyed wine was poured into each drinking glass. The lighting was soft with the glow of candles. A seemingly perfect evening had begun.

Dion smiled, giving himself a metaphorical pat on the head. How could Dionysius fail to understand Plato's wisdom in a setting such as this?

Lentil soup was brought around along with fried fish, sausages expertly browned, and raisins. The simple but delicious fare began a round of discussion surrounding the merits of fish versus poultry, which became a discussion of virtue versus vice, which inevitably turned to politics.

Plato was a foreigner, but he'd seen enough of the government of Syracuse to freely give an opinion when he was asked. "The Syracusan government system is imperfect at best," he said.

"What do you mean by that?" Dion asked.

Some of the others leaned forward on their couches, waiting to see how Plato would respond. If they were expecting a diplomatic answer from him, then their expectations were certainly violated.

"Well, let me explain," he said. "The way I see it, there are five types of government, and four of them are exceedingly unstable and difficult to maintain for any length of time.

"The first of the unstable types of government is the timocracy, or militaristic government. This is Sparta. This community is based on honor, but eventually war victories will lead to wealth, and the people will begin to equate honor with wealth. In this community, the rich rule and the poor are considered to be dishonorable."

"Are you saying that Sparta is doomed?" one of the guests asked.

"That is what I am saying. The more wars they win, the more wealth they will acquire, and the more they will look to fools with lots of money for their rule," Plato said.

"Are you saying that rich men are fools?" Dionysius asked.

"I'm simply saying that money becomes the deciding factor for ruling, so other factors like goodness and wisdom are no longer as important," Plato said. "The second unstable government is the oligarchy, which is the rule of a few rich people over the masses. Here the rich and poor who dwell together are pitted instinctively against each other. The poor will rise up against the ruling elite, but the rich, not wanting to give up their money to raise an army that would have to consist of the poor people, will have their hands tied.

"These poor will overthrow the oligarchy in order to set up a democracy, which is a rule by the people. This doesn't solve the problem of having the rich and the poor pitted against each other. They are still at odds, and now the poor have unrestrained liberty. They will become impatient with authority and so disorganized that no laws can settle them."

"What of Athens, then?" one guest asked. "Do you speak against your own city?"

"I love Athens as my own child, but I can acknowledge that the dangers I speak of are possible," Plato said. "An excess of anything usually leads to an excess of the very opposite thing. An excess of freedom leads to slavery. Poor men ruling their own city will see the rich plotting and pick their champion, who will rise up under the guise of a protector. He will vanquish the foe with the mobs that he has at his disposal, all the while hinting at promises for debt forgiveness and free land which he can't possibly keep. He might be driven out for a while, but he will come back a tyrant."

"So the fourth type of government is a tyranny?" Dion asked.

"Just so," Plato agreed, "and it is the worst. Tyrants lack reason in their judgments. His reason is enslaved by his thirst for power and wealth."

Dionysius had become noticeably uncomfortable at the turn the discussion had taken. "What are you trying to say?" he snapped at Plato, "And answer carefully."

"I'm saying simply that a state ruled by a tyrant whose lust for wealth and power has overshadowed his reason will rule over a state that is as enslaved as he is. No one keeps a tyrant's selfishness in check."

Dionysius slammed his hands on the table, jumping to his feet faster than he'd moved in years. "Are you implying that I am a selfish tyrant?" he yelled.

"If that's how you understand it, then no doubt you are correct," Plato said calmly.

Dionysius summoned his guards. "Take this man away," he said. "He blasphemes against me. Execute him. I never wish to see him alive again."

The guards pulled Plato from his couch, roughing him up as they did so, clearly expecting him to fight them.

From the other side of the table, Dion looked stricken. "You can't have him executed. Please don't do that," he pleaded.

"I never wish to see him again," Dionysius said, and the guards removed Plato from the room.

CHAPTER ELEVEN: PLATO FOUNDS THE ACADEMY

It took until they were out of earshot of the dining room for Plato to realize the swiftness with which his life had just changed. Surely they wouldn't kill him. It was a perfect example of what Plato had meant when he'd said that a tyrant's reason was enslaved by his selfishness. If he lived to found a school, this would certainly be an object lesson.

"Are you really going to execute me?" he asked.

The bigger guard turned to him. "All that matters to me is that the ruler never sees you again, so that I can keep my job and my house and family in tact. If you'd rather, I can sell you into slavery. I know of an Aeginian trader coming early tomorrow morning."

"That would be fine," Plato said. He'd have to come up with a way to contact friends in

Athens, but if the guards were willing to let him live, then it was a step in the right direction.

He was thrown into the prison a few blocks away. The cold stone building was empty except for Plato and one other man, a scraggly man who looked like he was in the final round of starvation.

"Do you think you could tell Dion what's to become of me?" Plato asked before the guard could walk away. "He'll want to know." He hoped that Dion would be able to at least contact his friends in Athens to come buy his freedom back.

"I don't know if I'll be in the mood to do favors for a slave."

"Tell him that Plato said to give you a bonus for your trouble."

The guard turned the lock and left without saying anything further.

The long night spent on the cold, damp floor left him exhausted the following morning.

A different guard came and kicked him to wake him up and brought him to a caravan leaving Syracuse today. His new master was a thick man who carried a switch. When Plato tried to converse with him, he only grunted and flicked the switch in Plato's direction to make him be quiet.

The next few weeks were spent in travel, during which time Plato was expected to feed the animals, clean the refuse off of his master's shoes, and bring him his supper. It wasn't so terrible. The man carried a switch, but he rarely used it and only when the livestock became belligerent. He almost never spoke, and when he did, a few foreign words at a time would issue forth from his mouth. Plato wondered if they even spoke the same language. He thought not.

As they prepared for the final day of travel before boarding a ship, a group of travelers slowed down in their wake as one man ran ahead to speak with Plato's master. Plato recognized him as Annicerus, one of his followers from

Athens. Money exchanged hands, and Plato's master freed him.

Plato climbed onto the extra horse that Annicerus and his company had brought. "That was an easy trade. How much did you have to pay him?" Plato asked, remembering that it had taken the guard of Dionysius quite a lot of haggling to agree on a price with the master.

"Twenty minae," Annicerus said.

Plato was taken aback. "That's far more than the guard who sold me got for me. No wonder it was a fast trade. I will reimburse you as soon as we arrive back at my family's estate."

"Consider it my tuition for a year at your new school," Annicerus said.

"My school? But I don't have a school."

"I received word from a man named Dion that you intend to start one."

Plato nodded. "I had thought of doing something like that. Perhaps getting kicked out of Syracuse and being sold into slavery was exactly the kick in the rear I needed to set things in motion."

"What will you call it?" Annicerus asked.

"I hadn't thought about it much." He was silent for a long moment as their horses kicked up dust around their heals, and the sun climbed higher in the sky.

387 BCE, Athens

Hundreds of years ago, twelve-year-old Helen of Troy was abducted by the Athenian king named Theseus, because she was beautiful and he was recently widowed. Helen's brothers, Castor and Pollux, were furious and decided to invade Athens in order to free their sister. They threatened Athens, saying that they planned to destroy the city. Academus approached them and begged them not to destroy the city if he told them where Helen had been hidden away. The brothers halted their attack on the city, and, finding their sister alive, spared Athens.

Academus was lauded as the hero and savior of Athens. On his land was planted a plantation of olive trees in his honor, and whenever the Lacedaemonians invaded Attica, this little piece of Athens was left untouched in honor of Academus.

That was the legend.

The piece of land Plato was to use for his school was a site that was sacred to the goddess, Athena, who was the goddess of wisdom. It was fitting. It was located about a mile from the north gate of the city of Athens on the same piece of land that was supposed to have belonged to Academus.

"I think I'll call it the Academy," Plato said, as he walked the property.

"The Academy," Annicerus said. "The hero of Athens on the land of the goddess of wisdom...that's fitting."

"I thought so," Plato said. He gazed out over the grove of olive trees and imagined sitting with a group of students in the shade of the leaves discussing deep philosophical concepts. It was his own little paradise on earth. He would start small, of course. If he found enough students, then he would contact his friends as well as some modern day celebrities to help him teach. He thought about who he might hire. The orators Demosthenes and Hyperides would be good fits, as would his sister's son, Speusippus if he was still interested in the idea.

Perhaps Eudoxus would be interested in teaching geometry. Geometry, Plato had decided, was very important to philosophy and reason. Once he built a structure, a sign above the door would read, "Let no one who cannot think geometrically enter."

Soon enough, his dream was a reality. The Academy wasn't a school in the strictest sense of the word. Plato didn't charge admissions fees or have a particular doctrine or curriculum that he taught to everyone. There wasn't a distinct separation between teachers and students, as Plato wanted to encourage learning and thought among all who went there. Such distinctions as the titles of junior and senior officers were given to indicate seniority.

He gained a modest number of students who came to talk about serious subjects or solved problems posed by Plato or any of the other teachers for the purpose of engaging their minds. Besides teaching and dialoging with students, Plato devoted a significant amount of his time to writing down his ideas in a form that was as familiar back then as it is now: the drama. His works featured men, and sometimes women, in conversation with each other about ideas and situations that were as many and varied as people themselves while also appealing to the sense of universality that comes with such seemingly basic concepts as beauty, truth, justice, goodness, and god.

Among the hundreds who would eventually flock to Athens to be Plato's students were two women, one by the name of Axiothea of Phlius and the other by the name of Lasthenia of Mantinea, both of whom came dressed as men and remained there even after Plato died and left the academy to his nephew, Speusippus. One of them was said to have been very beautiful when she was a teenager and full of an unstudied grace. They had each read the *Republic* and were eager to hear and learn more from its writer.

The Academy would go on to produce many successful alumni in the political field, though Plato himself wasn't much interested in practical politics.

The institution was founded on the idea that it was, indeed, possible for truth to be taught. This idea differed from what Socrates believed, that is, that moral knowledge and truth were based fundamentally on one's own inner reflection. The school was so popular that it would go on to be a famous gathering place for intellectuals interested in astronomy, philosophy, geometry, and mathematics for nine hundred years after Plato's death.

CHAPTER TWELVE: PLATO'S SECOND TRIP TO SYRACUSE

367 BCE, Syracuse

Plato could hardly believe that here he was back in Syracuse standing at the stoop of the man who had ordered him to be killed and then had him sold into slavery. Sometimes, Plato mused, it seemed that he had taken leave of his senses.

Several weeks earlier, Dion had sent him a message inviting him back to Syracuse, this time as a tutor to Dionysius II, his nephew who was the new tyrant of Syracuse. Plato would have turned the invitation down, but Dion had mentioned the phrase "philosopher king" in his message, which he knew would pique Plato's interest.

So, against his better judgment, here he was. Whatever had all gone down in Syracuse since he'd been thrown out all those years ago, it had to be an intriguing story. Obviously Dionysius I was dead. That's all Plato knew for sure.

A servant ushered Plato into an opulent sitting area. Dion rose from the couch where he sat. "I'm so glad you could make it back to visit me," he said, as though the circumstances of Plato's last visit had been pleasant and his departure entirely voluntary.

"Tell me, old friend. What has happened here since your brother-in-law had me killed?" Plato asked.

Dion laughed. "I love your humor, my friend. I knew you wouldn't hold a grudge. Well, you'll be happy to hear that my brother-in-law and I resolved our differences, in a manner of speaking."

"Will I?"

Dion chucked again, glancing down at his knees for a moment. "You see, he was too attached to having someone to take care of all of his government work, and I rather liked being paid to do so, so that's what we agreed on. He passed away a short time ago. While he was sick in bed, I tried to get him to discuss who his successor might be. I had hoped that he might be reasonable and hand the rule over to me. After all, I've been by his side taking care of his problems for many years."

Plato felt his eyebrows rising of their own accord. Dion always had that effect on him. He was a well-meaning man, but he could say some truly pompous things without realizing how self-centered he came off.

"Now I see what you're thinking, but you haven't met the son. He grew up cloistered in the acropolis because Dionysius I feared that someone might try to assassinate him and kill his heir. It wasn't a totally irrational fear. It happens to a lot of rulers we hear about, but even still. He should have given some mind to the boy's education. He's spent thirty years without discipline or any useful teaching. He has no knowledge of anything practical, let alone political, he doesn't know how to speak or to lead effectively, and that's not the worst of it." He leaned toward Plato, waiting for him to ask him the question.

"What's the worst of it?"

"He's set up his entire court with sorry excuses for young people. They know nothing about politics, and their high positions in court have gone straight to their heads. They get drunk and have sex with whomever they please wherever they please whenever they please, and they don't care who catches them. They carouse with prostitutes and chase after married women at night. They care nothing about honor or virtue and everything is a trivial joke to them." The old man had worked himself up until he was shaking.

"That sounds like too much for one state to bear."

"He killed his own father," Dion said, wringing his hands. "He heard me trying to persuade Dionysius to leave his rule to me. I left for a few minutes to relieve myself, and when I returned, the son was there, and the father was unconscious. I couldn't prove it, but I know he poisoned him. He never woke up. And now Syracuse is in the hands of an overgrown adolescent. You have to do something to help me."

Plato looked at the distraught old man. He'd been so composed only a few minutes ago, and now he'd been reduced to jitters.

"I'll see what I can do," Plato said, "but I wouldn't hold my breath if I were you. It sounds like I'm more likely to get thrown out again than I am to turn your nephew into anything resembling a philosopher king."

"I'll take whatever you can give," Dion said. "I've done the best I can, but he needs a lot more time than I have to give him. I think you will find that he is not altogether hopeless. He is not without intelligence."

Based on all his uncle had said about him, Plato was surprised to discover that Dionysius II seemed to be an amazingly receptive student. He listened to all that Plato taught him and quickly picked up on the various points he was trying to make.

Several months of tutoring had produced very positive changes in the younger Dionysius' behavior. Unfortunately, the same could not be said for his court, which behaved as licentiously as ever.

Some members of his council had persuaded him that Dion was trying to depose him. Dion did what he could to convince Dionysius that he was trying to do no such thing, but rumors circulated nonetheless, mostly by Dionysius' advisors who didn't like Dion and saw him as a threat to their own positions of power and wealth.

When Dionysius declared that he no longer wished to be a tyrant, the advisors were alarmed and renewed their efforts to bring Dion down. They didn't want their important offices to be given up for elections or drawn by lots among the citizens.

A letter between Dion and the Carthaginians was intercepted, and Dionysius' advisors persuaded him that Dion was aligned with Carthage, and they planned to overthrow him as ruler. Dionysius confronted Dion with the letter in hand and forced him into exile without giving him a chance to explain himself.

Some said that Aristomache, Dion's sister who was popular among the Syracusan people, was herself trying to take power.

Dionysius announced that Dion had gone to Athens for a while so that he couldn't stir up trouble in Syracuse. So while Plato was staying out of the blame game and confined to the acropolis in Syracuse, Dion was studying at the Academy and living it up with the upper crust of

Athens where the people loved him and treated him as something of a celebrity.

357 BCE, Athens

Syracuse seemed to be the gag gift that kept on giving. Plato had tried to leave multiple times, and each time he thought he'd gotten away, Dionysius had called him back to fix his public image by threatening Dion's life. Plato had gone, albeit reluctantly, but he hadn't been able to hold back his true opinions on the matter.

Offended and angry, Dionysius threw Plato in jail and, in a rage, sold all of Dion's property and kept the proceeds, made Dion's wife, Arete, marry his advisor, Timocrates, and immediately made sure that Dion knew about all of it.

The Athenian embassy got Plato out of jail and helped him escape back to Athens, by which point, Dion more closely resembled a boiling vat of fury than a man who'd gone from riches to rags.

Dion gathered supporters, and armed with a fleet and the knowledge that the Syracusans would gladly join a revolt if Dion could get into the city, he made for Syracuse. He spread rumors of attacks elsewhere in order to dilute Dionysius' troops. Then, he attacked. His attack was successful. Dionysius II was deposed, and Dion was elected as the new leader.

All seemed to be well, until the people realized that Dion was not interested in democracy. He told them that they were free and in the same breath told them how they were to use their freedom. Frustrated with him, they scared him out of Syracuse to the neighboring town of Leontini, where he was welcomed. The Syracusans called him back, however, when they found themselves under attack. He swept back in and saved them. He didn't win their hearts, but he stayed in Syracuse after that, until Calippus, a follower of his assassinated him as a follow through on a bribe he had taken from Dionysius II.

With that, Dion was gone, and Plato's involvement with the messy politics of Syracuse was over. The hope of a philosopher king in Syracuse would never come to fruition, which undoubtedly cast a gloom over the rest of Plato's career. He washed his hands of the whole mess and returned to his Academy, where he spent the rest of his life teaching and writing.

Some believe that he died in his sleep to the sound of a Thracian girl playing the flute. Others say that he died at a wedding. Regardless of whether or not he fell asleep at a wedding and died during a Thracian flute recessional, he was buried among the olive trees at his Academy.

CHAPTER THIRTEEN: ARISTOTLE AT THE ACADEMY

347 BCE Athens

It was a bittersweet time at the Academy. Plato had just been buried, and the leadership at the Academy had just changed hands. Aristotle wandered the peaceful groves of olive trees under the light drizzle.

He had come here as a student when he was seventeen. As a young boy, he had read some of Plato's dialogues and had been intrigued with the celebrated philosopher's ideas. Coming to Athens to hear him speak in person was a treat. He had stayed for twenty years, discussing all the latest science and philosophy in Plato's home or in the gymnasium of the Academy.

In spite of a rivalry with Isocrates' school that focused on training up wealthy, young politicians and making them experts in rhetoric, Plato's Academy continued to collect students and teachers. Isocrates claimed that Plato's school focused on ideas that were too abstract and otherworldly to be useful in society, but the evidence didn't support his accusation. In fact, the opposite was true. Plato's research Academy was the source of many of the most famous mathematicians, scientists, philosophers, politicians, and military strategists of the next nine hundred years.

Aristotle had hoped that Plato would have left the Academy to him when he was gone, but instead he'd left it to Speusippus, his sister's son.

Aristotle told himself that he was relieved. After all, the world was big, and he could go anywhere in it if he chose to now, provided he was careful.

Aristotle reflected on his experience at the Academy. Plato and his Academy had given him a good education—not full of sophistry like many of the day's educators in classical Athens.

Speeches were the lifeblood of Greek education and politics. The great Homeric heroes, Achilles and Odysseus, were known both for their great deeds and for their great words. Political power and getting projects done in Athens depended largely on effective public speaking.

Being able to give a great speech was more prized than having great ideas in Athens. Even a brilliant idea would be shot down if not presented simply, elegantly, and interestingly. The politicians who sat for the Athenian democracy had little to no specialized training and little patience for anything they didn't understand. Politicians had to have a good understanding of what their audience already knew and what they wanted to hear in order to deliver them a convincing speech.

A politician's goal was to know a little about a lot and to disguise how little he knew about a lot of things within eloquent rhetoric, an art form that the Sophists taught with eloquence.

Plato hadn't cared about beautiful speeches nearly as much as he had cared about finding truth.

Aristotle wondered, not for the first time, if this might be a good time to leave Athens for a while. Anti-Macedonian sentiment had grown in Athens, since King Philip II had switched his loyalty from Athens to Sparta in the Peloponnesian War. Since Aristotle was heavily connected with the Macedonian king, he was beginning to feel a little bit of trepidation every time he left his home. He was not, after all, an Athenian citizen. A lot of people didn't know of his connections, but there were some who would cause trouble if they thought they could talk their way out of it in front of a jury. Maybe politics were the real reason why Plato hadn't chosen him to take over the Academy.

Really, though, there were many likely reasons. Plato had been very attached to his theory of Forms and the idea that learning was simply the process of recognizing things that one already knows intrinsically. Aristotle was more inclined to believe that people didn't know everything intrinsically—that there were things that one only learned through the senses. He also had argued with Plato that there didn't have to be ideal forms of things when it was possible to plainly experience the reality of earthly things through the senses. For example, one didn't need to intrinsically understand the ideal form of a dog in order to see a dog in the street and observe its qualities.

Plato had allowed him to present his differing ideas to students, because he was fair-minded and always open to talking through anything, but it made sense that he didn't want the school to shift away from the Forms, as would inevitably happen under Aristotle's leadership.

Aristotle had always been interested in biology. His father, Nicomachus, had been the physician to the royal family of Macedonia, as well as a close friend to King Amyntas.

Nicomachus had taught his son a basic love for plants and animals before he'd died an untimely death when Aristotle was a young boy.

Aristotle stood looking north toward the city of his birth. Stagira was a small seaport town on the north coast of Greece in the center of Macedonia. Last year, King Philip had occupied the little town and destroyed it. Word had it that there was very little left of Stagira. He hadn't seen the place since he'd left it twenty years ago to come to Athens, but somehow it still made him sad to know that a piece of his history was gone, perhaps forever.

The moments slipped away until Aristotle felt a presence to his left. It was Xenocrates, a mathematician and close friend of Plato's.

"It's a sad sort of day," Xenocrates said.

Aristotle nodded.

"I understand how you feel. I had hoped for the Academy as well."

Aristotle nodded. Xenocrates had wanted to lead it more than any of the teachers at the school.

"Are you interested in taking a trip with me?" Xenocrates asked. "I'm thinking of going to visit Hermias of Atarneus. In fact, I've almost entirely made up my mind to go, but I have no wish to travel alone." Hermias was a friend to both of them. He had come to Plato's Academy to study years ago.

Aristotle thought about it for a moment and then answered slowly, as was his habit. "Yes, I think I would like to do that. In fact, I know I would. When are you leaving?"

"I'm thinking to leave in three days. That should give us both the time we need to prepare and let the others know that we'll be gone."

Aristotle nodded. "Then it's decided."

347 BCE, Assos

Aristotle and Xenocrates arrived at Assos and met Hermias with great excitement. They had heard all the rumors of his wealth and success and were eager to see how true they were. He'd originally been the Bithynian slave of Eubulus, who had been a wealthy banker as well as a tyrant over all of the lands that surrounded Assos and Atarneus. Though Hermias was his slave, Eubulus respected him and had sent him to Plato's Academy for a while to learn. Upon returning to Atarneus after his education, Hermias helped Eubulus rule his commercial towns.

Hermias had won his freedom, and, when Eubulus died, all of his wealth and property had been left to the former slave.

Hermias came out and greeted his two friends. "I hate to throw this on you the moment you arrive," Hermias said, when they'd had their greetings, "but King Philip heard that you were coming, and he wants to speak with you."

Aristotle had heard that Hermias and King Philip had been at odds for some time now. It made sense that they might both appreciate Aristotle's historic connection with the temperamental monarch who wanted to use Hermias' land as a jumping off point for his much longed for campaign to Thrace and Persia. After King Philip had torn down his hometown, Aristotle wasn't predisposed to do him any favors, but he didn't imagine he had much of a choice in the matter. He'd have to at least see the king.

"Yes. Er," Hermias said. "That is to say, King Philip is waiting for you in my sitting room. He's been here all day, and I've long since run out of things to say to him. I'm sorry to throw this on you. I know you're tired."

Aristotle resisted the urge to throttle his friend, reminding himself that King Philip pretty much did what he wanted, even if a homeowner passive aggressively told him to stop camping out in his living room. Today was the day to talk to King Philip, apparently.

Aristotle entered the sitting room. King Philip immediately jumped to his feet and boomed a welcome. "I remember when we used to play together at the palace as youngsters."

Aristotle regarded the slightly younger man with reserve, a little unsure of how his next words would be taken. The young king reputedly had a ravenous temper, but, in this case, Aristotle had access to something he wanted, that being an alliance with Hermias. "I remember when you destroyed my hometown last year," he said.

King Philip looked at him blankly for a moment before he remembered what he had done. "Oh. Stagira. I remember. Yes. Well. Unfortunate story there. It couldn't be helped. I'm sure you understand."

"You are, perhaps, too generous with my understanding. Have I torn down the walls of your family palace and enslaved your household?"

"I am sorry that it had to happen," the king said, looking apologetic, but most probably because it meant that it was currently causing him to have an inconvenient conflict with Aristotle. "I can make it up to you. Name a price, and I will pay it."

"Rebuild Stagira and free its people from their bondage," Aristotle said.

"I can't do that at present." Seeing Aristotle's face, he backpedaled. "How about I look into it. I'll see if there's anything to be done about it. In the meantime, how about this." He named a large price.

"I will think about it," Aristotle said. "If I decide to take you up on your offer, you will have to promise that what you did in Stagira won't happen here in Assos or Atarneus or in any of Hermias' towns."

"Of course," King Philip said, eager to make the deal.

"I'm not going to decide today," Aristotle said. "I've just arrived from a long journey, and I wish to rest. So if that is all, then I will leave you now."

"Of course," the king said.

Aristotle left the room.

He had always liked Philip, even if he was prone to causing huge destruction and then thinking through all of the ramifications later when he realized that suddenly everyone was mad at him. He was confident that he would get Hermias to see the wisdom of having King Philip as an ally, especially with Persia constantly breathing down his neck to get after his land. After all, he had no army of his own, only untrained residents who would probably fight either for Hermias or Persia, depending on who promised the better deal and seemed more likely to win.

Persia had had several years of incompetent rulers under whom civil war and other internal conflicts had made war against anyone else nearly impossible. Now with Artaxerxes III Ochus as the emperor, Persia was straightening itself out and looking for the next land to conquer and annex into its empire.

Yes, Macedon and its army would be a good ally for Hermias to have. The alliance itself might be enough to keep Persia looking elsewhere for conquest.

CHAPTER FOURTEEN:
ARISTOTLE'S QUEST FOR NEW
KNOWLEDGE

346 BCE, Assos

Aristotle entered the garden where he often passed the afternoon with Hermias and a handful of other men interested in long discussions about philosophy, science, and ethics. He breathed the fresh scent of the leaves and blossoms, marveling at how quickly time passed. The buds of yesterday were luscious flowers today, and tomorrow they would fall off and be trampled. That's how it seemed anyway.

Today he had been thinking about something Hermias had done earlier. He'd taken livestock from one of his subjects in order to serve his own guests the best livestock in the land. The subject had given in to the demand, but it was clear by the look on his face that he hadn't been pleased to do so. Aristotle had hung back and talked with the subject, a man whose daughter was getting married soon. The fattened livestock had been intended for her wedding feast.

Hermias couldn't have known that, but if he had, would it have made a difference? Was it right for Hermias to demand something that belonged to one of his subjects?

"What are you mulling over today, my friend?" Hermias asked.

Aristotle stood studying the petals of a magenta blossom. He thought for a moment, wondering how to bring up the subject. "I'm thinking about the way you took the cow from that man and his family earlier today," he said finally, deciding that being direct was the best way to go about his questions.

"King Philip is coming for dinner tonight," Hermias said. "I needed to present him with my best. He is a king."

"The cow was meant for the man's daughter's wedding feast."

Hermias frowned. "I think the king is more important than a commoner's wedding."

"But you didn't take the cows for the king, you took them for yourself, so that you could look good in front of the king."

Hermias said nothing to that.

"Having grown up with King Philip when he was a young prince, I can assure you that the king won't notice the difference between the best livestock and the second best livestock."

"It's the principle of the thing. He's the king, so he's not to get only the second best."

"Tell me, Hermias, what did you give the man in return for the use of his livestock," Aristotle said.

"He has my good favor, of course. I shall remember that he gave me his best cow when it comes time to bestow honors or grant awards."

"I doubt he sees it that way."

"Why shouldn't he?" Hermias said.

"For starters, you didn't ask him for it; you mandated that he should bring it to you," Aristotle said.

"Are you saying that you think I should have said please and thank you?"

Aristotle was quiet for a moment. He needed a new angle, because Hermias was too caught up in his own logic to see any other from this position. It was in moments like these that he wished he had the quick brilliance that Plato had possessed. He had an answer ready for everything and could come up with brilliant arguments and questions on the spot. Instead, Aristotle was logical and methodical. Answers came to him, but often long after he needed them.

"Let's pretend for a moment that you are King Philip's subject, and he comes to you and demands that you give him your best piece of land with sweet grass that runs along a fresh stream. It is the piece of land that feeds your cattle so that your household doesn't go hungry.

It's also where your young niece goes to play and sit on her favorite rock. If you are his subject, then you have no choice but to give it to him, but how will you feel about it?" Aristotle said.

A few men had entered the garden while he spoke and sat down on the benches by the fountain to listen.

"What did he give me in return for it?" Hermias asked.

"Nothing but his goodwill."

"I would be angry. He has much more land than I do, and he hasn't given me anything in return for it," Hermias said, frowning.

"Would you go to your neighbors and tell them about the injustice the king has brought against you and your family?"

"Certainly."

"So now let's say that King Philip goes to war against Persia, and his armies are being annihilated. He comes to your doorstep desperate for your help, because he's one attack away from losing everything. You have the opportunity to let him in and offer whatever protection and services you have at your disposal or turn him over to the Persians for a reward. What would you feel most inclined to do?"

"Well, I guess it would serve him right if I shut my door in his face. If he's about to lose a war against Persia, then he won't be around to punish me for it. Maybe I'd let him in and give him over to the Persian king in order to win favor with King Artaxerxes in hopes of preserving my household that way."

"You are King Philip," Aristotle said.

Hermias frowned more deeply, lines creasing his forehead.

"Perhaps obtaining the cow for yourself in order to please King Philip is a worthy end, but I think it's nobler to keep the favor of your people, that you might be revered as a fair and just ruler, rather than as a self-serving tyrant."

Hermias thought about this for a long moment. "I think you're right," he finally said. "The cow has already been slaughtered. What do you propose that I do to make this right?"

"That is up to you," Aristotle said, "but I'd suggest that it be a great enough payment to make up for the price of the cow as well as any ill feelings created between you."

Hermias went out to his own large herd of livestock and chose the best from among them. Then he ordered that the small herd be brought to the man whose cow he had taken. The way he figured, even if none of these were quite as good as the one that had already been slaughtered for dinner, there were enough of them to triple the man's own herd or bring him several years' wages at market if he sold them.

The formerly angry subject, seeing what the despotic ruler had done to repay him, sent him several baskets of fresh, ripe fruit from his orchards that fall and invited him to his daughter's wedding celebration.

Hermias was excited by the prospect of being a beloved master of his people and thereafter spent many hours in conversation with Aristotle and his friends about ethics and politics learning how to better ingratiate himself with his people.

The territory under his rule grew to include much of the countryside along the coast. Hermias was pleased with Aristotle's advice and offered him his niece as his wife when she came of age, an offer which Aristotle accepted, having come to appreciate the young girl's mind and interest in science, especially in biology and embryology. Despite her young age, the two would always have something to talk about, and Aristotle found that there wasn't anyone he'd rather marry than Pythias. For a woman, she was very agreeable, and perhaps proof that the Greeks weren't allowing women to live up to their full potential when it came to being productive members of society.

345 BCE, Mytilene, Lesbos

Aristotle had always been interested in biology, and when his friend, Theophrastus mentioned an interest in going to Lesbos, which had been his homeland before going to Plato's school in Athens many years ago, Aristotle was eager to join him in studying the fauna on the island.

He went with his new wife, Pythias, to Lesbos, the sunniest island in Greece known for its greenness and vast array of plant life. There, he spent the next couple of years studying and dissecting living things in order to learn about them and classify them. His classification system was the first known attempt at categorizing all the different types of life on earth.

Unlike those before him, Aristotle sought not only to differentiate the actions and functions of each animal but to put them into a hierarchical ranking based on the degree to which an organism showed the ability to move and stay alive.

He separated organisms into categories that he called "animals with blood," and "animals without blood." The animals with blood were broken down further by differentiating between those that gave birth to live offspring and those that gave birth to eggs, which hatched their offspring. The animals without blood he divided into non-shelled, cephalopods, and shelled. By observing the fish brought in by fishermen, he was able to determine that there was a difference between fish and aquatic mammals.

All in all, he classified around five hundred different species of fish, birds, and mammals.

Though modern scientists have redefined the categories as vertebrates and invertebrates rather than with and without blood (due to the fact that some invertebrates do have blood, though it looks different), much of Aristotle's classification system was left in tact through the nineteenth century.

Unlike scientists today, Aristotle was concerned with the nature of the intellectual purposes and the soul in living things. By soul, he simply meant the form that certain matter takes, which allows it certain types of motion, whether that is the ability to grow or the ability to compare other forms with each other. He said that the plants, animals, and people were different from each other because of the kind of soul that each possessed. The extent to which a thing fulfills its purpose relates to ethics. Ethics, to Aristotle, was entirely connected with biology.

Plants had a vegetative soul, which was in charge of growth and reproduction. Animals had a vegetative soul as well as a sensitive soul, which dictated the senses and the ability for motion. Humans, which were superior to the other forms of life, possessed a vegetative, sensitive, and rational soul, which meant that they alone were capable of thinking and reflecting on all else around them.

Aristotle was able to give an account of the reproductive embryonic growth of chickens by taking fertilized eggs and breaking them open at different intervals in order to observe when and where a chicken embryo's organs start visibly developing.

He was also interested in thinking about the reasons for an animal's parts. For example, he noted that some creatures with weak, dull teeth had multiple stomachs and surmised that the multiple stomachs were to make up for the lack of sharp teeth. Nature, he said, always wanted to preserve some sort of balance in the world.

Some of Aristotle's own scientific research was surprising cogent for the fourth century, BCE, but plenty of his work, especially his scientific writings based on myths, remind us that not all of his work can be taken as fact.

CHAPTER FIFTEEN: ARISTOTLE RETURNS TO MACEDON

343 BCE, The Macedonian Palace

For the first time since he'd left home at the age of seventeen, Aristotle stood in the Macedonian palace. The coolness of the stone wall under his hand chilled him. A lot had happened since the last time he'd stood in this doorway looking out into the courtyard.

Aristotle stepped into the quiet warmth of the garden cloistered in the center of the palace. He was here for a new job. King Philip had hired him to be the head of the royal school of Macedon, which would include tutoring his son, Alexander. The king had told him that Alexander was intelligent and eager to learn. Aristotle wondered briefly if those were the words of a proud father or a statement of fact. He would find out soon enough.

Normally, he would have been excited to get the opportunity to train Macedon's future king, but tonight he was tired. Tonight he wanted to look at the leaves on the trees and let his mind wander aimlessly along their veins. He found himself thinking, as he often did that it was always strange how the world could go on after death. It was equal parts frightening and reassuring to see that nature remained constant no matter who was there to look at it.

He wondered, not for the first time, about the nature of the soul. Plato had believed that the body and the soul were separable at death. Aristotle wasn't sure about that. He was beginning to believe that a soul was to the body what sight was to the eye. There didn't seem, unfortunately, to be a way to scientifically figure out if there was a separation between the body, the soul, and the intellect. That was the mystery of death.

Unless a body were to come alive after being dead and give an account of the soul, it was impossible to truly know the relationship between the two in this life.

A rustle behind him broke up his thought, and he turned to see who had joined him in the garden. A young boy stood outside the doorway, hesitating.

"It's okay," Aristotle said. "Come out and sit down. I'm thinking about the body and the soul."

The boy practically bounced across the courtyard, his whole body radiant with energy.

"What about the body and soul?" the boy asked.

"Do you think the soul and the body are like two halves of a person or do you think they are the form and the function of a person?" Aristotle asked.

"What's form and function?"

Aristotle explained the metaphor of the eye. The eye was the form; seeing was the function.

"So the body is the form, and the soul is the function."

"Exactly so."

The boy screwed his face up in thought. "If the soul is like seeing, then a soul can't keep on living without its body."

"That's certainly true."

"So when a body dies, the soul dies too," the boy said. "But I'd rather believe that the soul can live forever. If the soul is one half of a person, then there's a better chance that it leaves the body and keeps living after the body dies."

"That certainly sounds nicer, I suppose."

They sat in silence for a moment. Then the boy asked, "Which is the truth?

Aristotle smiled. "No one knows."

"That's annoying."

"Yes, but it's interesting to think about," Aristotle said. "I don't believe we've been introduced yet."

"I'm Alexander," the boy said, incredulous that anyone could be in his home and not know who he was. "Who are you?"

"I am your new tutor."

Alexander proved to be an avid learner. Whatever reluctance he might have felt upon first commencing his studies with Aristotle, he soon set them aside as he began to understand how knowledge was the key to all the things he wanted out of life.

He read Homer's *Illiad* over and over, feeling that it must be the handbook of all military virtues. Along with Homer, he read the *History* by Philistus, the plays of Aeschylus,

Euripides, and Sophocles, and some poetry by Telestes and Philoxenus.

Alexander and Aristotle became fond of each other, both possessing a zest for learning and thinking and minds for logic and strategizing. Alexander knew that he would be king one day and took that very seriously. He wanted to hear what Aristotle thought about various strategies and conquests. Aristotle was very much in favor of Alexander expanding the Macedonian kingdom into the east.

Aristotle told him that he should lead the Greeks with justice and lead the barbarians as a tyrant. He advised Alexander to think of the barbarians as little better than animals or plants, which lacked the ability for rational thought, and to care for the Greeks as he would his own relations and friends. Aristotle was very pro-Greek, and he wasn't afraid that Alexander should know and share his opinions.

While he was the head of the royal school of Macedonia, Aristotle also tutored Ptolemy and

Cassander, who would, like Alexander, go on to become kings.

341 BCE, Macedonia

Aristotle was frustrated with the king and more than a little afraid for his friend, Hermias. King Philip had decided to withdraw his support from Hermias' land, because Athens and Persia had threatened to attack Macedonia if King Philip continued with his plans to take over Asia Minor.

The sudden lack of protection from Macedonia meant that the Persian ruler finally had access to Hermias' land. Artaxerxes sent a mercenary to Hermias to try to learn about the Macedonian plans for possible invasion as well as to gain back the land he'd lost due to revolts.

Aristotle wrote the mercenary one letter after another urging him to switch sides and support Hermias. Seeing a way into Hermias' home, the mercenary agreed. Once he'd won

Hermias' trust and gained his support, he seized him, locked him in chains, and dragged him to Susa.

There, the mercenary tortured him under the direction of Artaxerxes. Artaxerxes had intended to extract from him King Philip's plans for invasion, but it didn't work.

Word had come to Aristotle through friends that the man's dying words had been, "I have done nothing unworthy of philosophy."

Aristotle had been moved to write a hymn in his honor and to dedicate a statue to him in the religious center of the world, Delphi.

Aristotle stood in the garden at the palace, stricken with grief at the loss of his friend. He wanted to let himself feel the sting of his friend's tragic demise for a moment. He wondered if Philip regretted pulling his support or if he considered it to be a necessary evil. The thought that the latter might very well be the case sickened him, and he resolved to think, for this moment, only about philosophy and a brighter future rather than the grim political landscape of the present.

October, 336 BCE, Macedonia

Aristotle had heard the rumors circulating the palace of someone possibly trying to assassinate King Philip. Such rumors weren't uncommon. Considering the array of competing wives he'd had, maybe it was most shocking that they weren't more frequent.

His most recent marriage to Cleopatra Eurydice of Macedon, his seventh wife, had passions in the court running high, as the new wife's uncle had remarked that maybe now Philip would be able to have a legitimate heir. This was in reference to the fact that Alexander's mother, Olympias, was not Macedonian.

Alexander, furious, had thrown his wine glass at the man and shouted at him. King Philip, drunk from the wedding feast, stood and drew his sword. He charged at Alexander and promptly fell over on his face from his drunkenness.

"Look at this man. He's getting ready to cross from one continent to another and here he can't even cross from one table to another without falling on his face," Alexander shouted. He'd taken his mother and escaped from the country for a while until ire on all sides cooled and he was allowed to return to Macedonia.

Aristotle left his bedchamber one morning sometime later feeling that something terrible might happen today. Today was the second day of the wedding celebration of Philip's daughter, Cleopatra, and the prince Alexander of Epirus.

While he was entering the theater, King Philip passed between his son, Alexander, and his brand new son-in-law, Alexander of Epirus. At first it looked like the young nobleman,

Pausanias, was merely leaning forward to touch the king's back.

Then, the king fell forward on his face, this time not from drunkenness but because of the dagger that stuck out of his back.

Pausanias bolted from the procession. He might have gotten away, except that he tripped over the heavy rug covering the floor at the entrance to the theater. Alexander's friends grabbed the assassin and put a sword through him, killing him instantly.

By the time the story reached Aristotle's ears, a number of theories had also been fabricated about the person who had instigated the assassination. Some said that Pausanias had been angry with King Philip for denying him a request for justice against wife number seven's uncle, Attalus, who was a cruel man. Some said that Olympias was getting revenge on King Philip for casting her aside and wanted to ensure that her own son would be the next king of Macedon. Some accused Alexander himself for killing his father, saying that it explained why Alexander's friends had killed Pausanias immediately instead of capturing him and forcing him to tell who was behind the assassination.

In any case, King Philip and his assassin were both dead, and if someone else was to blame for it, whoever it was wasn't talking about it.

CHAPTER SIXTEEN: ARISTOTLE FOUNDS THE LYCEUM

335 BCE, Athens

As Alexander, son of Philip, was crowned as king of Macedon at the young age of twenty, Aristotle started to feel that his time in Macedon was at a close. His students were grown and moving forward with careers, and he sensed that his presence and opinions would not be welcomed.

As much as he had come to love Alexander like a son, he knew that they disagreed in many things. Where Alexander could be impulsive and prone to fits of temper, Aristotle was collected and methodical in nearly everything he did. Then there was the matter of dealing with the Persian Empire. Aristotle knew that Alexander's mother, Olympias, had made him believe that it was his destiny to make himself the king of the Persians. She was an incredibly ambitious woman, not at all the invisible Athenian housewife, but a politician in her own right.

Aristotle feared for the young man who wanted so desperately to outdo his father that Aristotle wondered what brash things he might try in battle. He might make his dream a reality if he succeeded and get himself killed if he didn't. He certainly had boundless optimism. Hopefully that wouldn't work against him.

His mind made up, Aristotle packed his things and left Macedon for good.

After many years of travel, politics, and teaching in schools across the land, Aristotle finally decided that it was a good time to return to teaching in Athens. He didn't wish to return to Plato's Academy and instead decided to found his own school of philosophy.

For his school he found an old gymnasium named for Apollo Lyceus. Many philosophers had historically used the space to give public lectures, including Plato at one time. Aristotle began a new program of study there that would teach students in all of the new scientific research he had obtained abroad.

His interest in scientific learning sparked an interest in creating a program that would promote cooperative research in the sciences. He continually added to his library of philosophical and scientific writings so that his students would have a vast array of research at their disposal. He assigned his students research projects that were sometimes historical and sometimes scientific in nature that served the purpose of group as well as individual learning.

He lectured in the mornings and then went out onto the Lyceum's grounds to lecture to the public. He did many of his lectures as he walked around the Lyceum's grounds.

Aristotle's Lyceum was in part student led. He encouraged his students to elect an administrator to meet with the faculty leaders at ten-day intervals. It was important to him that his students were allowed to experience leadership and get involved in their own education.

Perhaps the most remarkable part about Aristotle's Lyceum was in his development of the first ever zoo and botanical garden, which aided students in their study of plants and animals. He often retired there in the evenings to think through difficult concepts or mull over a problem he was having.

325 BCE

When Aristotle's wife, Pythias, had died, he'd felt a little lost. Pythias had been quiet, constant, and intelligent, certainly not the nagging shrew Socrates had reputedly married. He was genuinely sad to have lost her, though he sought comfort in watching their young daughter, also named Pythias, grow up.

But time had gone on, and he'd found surprising comfort in one of Pythias' maids, a woman by the name of Herpyllis, who was also from Aristotle's hometown of Stagira. She was older than Pythias had been and more confident in herself and her capabilities. The first time they were intimate, Aristotle was surprised to discover that she was far more exuberant about sex than Pythias had been. She liked to make love as much as he did and maybe more, a fact that excited him nearly as much as breakthroughs in his writings and studies.

Aristotle was pleased when Herpyllis told him that she was expecting his child. He was hoping for a son.

They had a son, and Aristotle named him Nicomachus after the baby's late grandfather, Aristotle's father.

Around this time, Aristotle carried on a flirtation with a young man by the name of Palaephatus of Abydus, who was a historian of the day. A man getting up there in years should have the pleasure of youth to surround himself with, he felt. Palaephatus made him feel the bliss of youth for brief moments, which made their time together precious.

During his later years at the Lyceum, Aristotle composed many of his writings. Sadly, not many of them have made it to the light of today's era, though record of their existence and circulation is present in the historical accounts from Aristotle's contemporaries.

Besides his work in building the foundations of modern scientific enquiry, Aristotle accomplished many other important things for the world of philosophy as well. He was the first one to create the formalized logical structure, which was known as the syllogism.

If X is Y and B is X, then B is Y. The syllogism is a simple deduction from two premises to form a conclusion. His most famous example in history is: "All men are mortal. Socrates is a man. Therefore, Socrates is mortal."

He deduced that the ability to reason puts humans at the top of the hierarchical animal structure. None of the animals he'd studied over the years, after all, had fit the things around them into such complicated, abstract structures as people.

322 BCE, Chalcidice

As time went on, Aristotle grew estranged from Alexander the Great. Some of the estrangement was due to their distance. Aristotle never returned to Macedonia, and Alexander was busy campaigning across Greece and Asia Minor. Some say that they had a falling out because of Alexander's determination to conquer the Persians. It's very possible that Aristotle was disapproving of some of Alexander's military strategies.

Rumors reached him that Alexander, once equal parts intellectual and impulsive, had fallen victim to his delusions of grandeur, becoming prey to paranoia and megalomania.

A legend from antiquity circulated saying that Aristotle had a hand in Alexander's death, but there is no proof of this anywhere in history.

When the death of Alexander the Great reached Athens, Aristotle knew that he would not be safe staying there. If the Macedonian Empire was about to come crashing down, then no Macedonian born person was going to be safe in Athens.

Leaving the Lyceum in the hands of Theophrastus, he fled along with his family to his mother's home in Chalcidice. Eurymedon the Hierophant had accused him of not showing due respect to the gods of Athens, and it would be only a matter of time before he was called before the government of Athens and sentenced to death. He was not, after all, an Athenian citizen and had no rights to a trial or a defense.

He wondered when he fled how many days he had left to live. He was an old man now, and he was feeling his age. He had no wish to pass the last few days on earth in a prison cell, uncomfortable and cold with hunger and fear. He famously said that he refused to allow the Athenians to sin a second time against philosophy, remembering tales of Socrates' death of poisoning in a prison cell. Though he'd spent many years in Athens getting an education and teaching the next generation of young people, it was still not his city the way it had been for Socrates. He had no wish to die for a city that wasn't his.

Some months later the hills around his home in Chalcidice were green and steep. His bedroom window looked out upon the phthalo blue water that danced and sparkled under the sun's approval. Shadows wavered under the surface of the clear water indicating where the deepest parts of the sea began. He'd watched this scene from his bed for many days in a row, having become too weak and tired to get up anymore. Soon he would have an eternity to rest. Now he was content to wait quietly for Herpyllis to bring him his dinner and tell him of the latest antics their son, Nicomachus, had been up to.

Herpyllis came in, as if his thoughts had summoned her. She held a bowl in her hand and spooned the soup into his mouth. He swallowed like a diligent patient until the contents of the bowl were finished.

She set the bowl aside and sat with him on the bed. He traced her forearm slowly and methodically, appreciating the softness of the inside of her wrist contrasted with the hardness of her hands. They were hands that were used to labor and wrists that were strong from lifting and washing. Even though Aristotle had long since told her that she didn't need to continue to do the household chores herself, she preferred to do them anyway. She said that she liked the rhythm and purpose of having daily tasks to perform and check off the mental list.

"Let me get Nicomachus," she whispered. "He will want to say goodbye to you."

Aristotle smiled sadly. Wherever he was going after death, he felt sure that he would miss his little son who had been the light of his life during his short time in the world.

Herpyllis carried the chubby toddler into the room. Aristotle patted the little boy's hair as the boy threw himself onto his father's lap.

"Be careful son," Herpyllis said. "You don't want to hurt father."

"It's okay," Aristotle said. "He can't hurt me." He listened to his son jabber in his babyish language until he started to feel himself sinking into a deep fatigue. It was different from the fatigue he'd felt for the past few weeks. This felt like a cerulean ocean current that would overtake him and pull him gently into the afterlife.

He was awake enough to note that someone was taking Nicomachus out of the room. He looked into Herpyllis' kind face one last time and then put the last bit of energy into turning his face to watch the sea as he drifted into whatever came next.

Having named his friend, Antipater as the chief executor of his will, Aristotle slipped away quietly in safety and comfort later that night, finally finding the answer to the question of the relationship between the soul and the body that all of us will someday learn as well.

CHAPTER SEVENTEEN: RELIGION IN ATHENS

The Gods of Olympus

At the beginning of time, Chaos existed alone in the void. Then Erebus, who was the place of night and death appeared, fabricated from nothing. Chaos and Erebus gave birth to Love, Light, and Gaea. Many complicated liaisons later, Gaea, who was the earth, gave birth to the sky and named him Uranus, who also became her husband and surrounded her on all sides.

Gaia and Uranus produced the twelve Titans who went on to fight against the Olympians, among them, Zeus. After a series of violent acts, Zeus, who was the cupbearer on Mount Olympus, was the victor over the Titans, imprisoning all of them except Atlas, who was forced to hold the earth on his shoulders for the rest of time.

Zeus secured his power by killing the great monster, Typon, which Gaia had sent at him as revenge for imprisoning her children, the Titans. He further secured his leadership over all of the gods by winning a challenge against the Giants and vanquishing them.

Entire books are filled with the violent, erotic, twisted, unjust dealings of the Greek gods, and there's not space even to summarize the long history of emasculations, battles, and illicit sex that makes up the bizarre world of Greek mythology. Looking at the gods and goddesses and their dealings with each other and all of the irrational superstitions held by the Athenians can have a tendency to make us feel as though we would have had nothing in common with them.

Is it any wonder that with these kinds of role models Athens itself could be violent, erotic, and twisted in kind? Then again, maybe the gods are merely a reflection of human nature and its longings and conflicts, and human nature hasn't changed one iota in 2400 years.

Religion in Athens didn't look that much different than it does in many first world countries today. Some people held with the traditional beliefs of the Homeric heroes and the gods of Olympus. There were Zeus and Hera and their offspring, and most Greek city-states had these in common. Some people adopted less superstitious beliefs about the traditional Olympian gods, subduing some of the madness of the religion. Some joined other cultures' religions or cults, like the Orphic cult or other Mystery cults. Others became atheists and agnostics.

Socrates was blamed both for worshipping gods other than those of the state and for being an atheist, accusations that he died for, though he never claimed to be an atheist.

Atheistic and agnostic citizens had be very careful with whom they shared their beliefs, especially since not participating in religion in Athens was to not participate in the politics of the community, which was considered to be a grave offense.

Religion was tied to politics in that to be a citizen of a city, one was expected to uphold and participate in the religious practices and festivals of the city. Religion wasn't a private, personal experience; it was a corporate experience. Failure to participate in religious ceremonies and customs was a failure to participate in the community in a respectful way. The democracy of Athens would have been confused and angered by our idea of the separation of church and state, or of religion and politics.

Because religion was so intertwined with every other aspect of a person's life, the state could prosecute someone even for the things they chose to do in the privacy of their own home. It wasn't an issue of fairness or individual privacy; it was an issue of piety for the benefit of the land. Impiety could result in the gods' anger and punishment, which was almost always corporate. When nature performed a great feat—

a storm, a flood, or a fire—it wasn't just an act of god to the Athenians. It *was* a god.

There was no shortage of religious choices in Athens, and many chose to worship any combination of native and foreign gods just to make sure they were covered. With very little scientific understanding of the way the world works, the people felt that they were at the whim of hundreds of fickle gods who might become angry or spiteful on a moment's notice. Worship was done corporately as well as privately with one's family, and it was done largely through ritualistic animal sacrifices with rigid stipulations. The task of every Athenian was to keep the gods smiling on them.

There were local gods unique to each city and national gods who were more or less the same between cities. Some gods, like Aphrodite, had two temples in Athens, one of which belonged to a local cult, and the other of which belonged to an older tradition. Local religious customs varied from one town to the next, but the overarching story of Olympus remained the same, intertwining religion with the very history of the land and the people.

A Private Sacrifice

The Greeks primarily communicated with the gods through burnt sacrifices. Sometimes the sacrifices were as small as a dove or a bun from the baking thrown on the fire. Sometimes the sacrifice was a big as an ox, especially if it was as a community festival or supplication.

When an individual wanted to perform a sacrifice of thanksgiving in his home, he would usually invite some friends as witnesses. A piglet or other small animal would be held still by a slave next to the altar. Friends and family would gather around the altar. The host would put a burning torch into a bowl of water and then sprinkle the water on his guests to purify them. He then would sprinkle the water on the head of the sacrifice. The water would cause the animal to nod its head instinctively, which was taken as an agreement to be sacrificed.

The knife would be taken from the basket and used to slice the animal's throat. The women would scream to give voice to the animal, and the blood would be caught in a bowl. A portion of the meat would be burnt on the altar to the god, and the rest would be carried away by the slave to be cooked. At that point, the party would begin for the family and the guests. Times of sacrifice were the usually the only times the Greeks ate meat.

Foreign, Newfangled, Unwanted Ideas

Orphism was an offshoot of the worshippers of Dionysus. The myth of Dionysus goes as follows: Zeus and Persephone have a child named Dionysus, and Zeus leaves his throne and inheritance to the child. Hera becomes angry with Zeus for having a child with another goddess. She and the Titans trick Dionysus while Zeus is away, and they kill him and eat him, with the exception of his heart, which Hera keeps and gives to Zeus when he returns. Furious, Zeus strikes the Titans with a thunderbolt, and the ashes from their remains become the mortal bodies of human beings that hold our divine souls in prison.

The beliefs of Orphism held that people were reincarnated until they reached initiation into the orgies of Dionysus and became free from their bodies. These reincarnations were said to happen in cycles of ten. They believed that humans had both divine and earthly origins, having been created from the blood of the heart of a slain Dionysus and the ashes of the Titans. Denial of bodily desire was the only way to purify the divine soul and succeed in freeing it from the body's prison.

To most people, science wasn't an important subject of study, but by the end of the Classical Era, people like Aristotle were starting to take an interest in learning how the world works in a practical, rather than merely theoretical, way.

Xenophanes provided the arguments used by atheists and agnostics that taking the gods out of the minutiae of everyday life allowed people to notice patterns in nature. Aristotle noted that a rock always, rather than episodically, fell downwards. Xenophanes said that using the gods to explain every natural occurrence prevented people from forming any understanding of the way the world worked in order to better themselves.

Socrates also argued that if the gods were real, their sexual flings and assaults were immoral on a human level and decidedly ungod like. He finally noted that each cultural group created gods in its own image.

CHAPTER EIGHTEEN: AN INTIMATE LOOK AT MALE SEXUALITY IN ATHENS

In classical Athens, as with any civilization, love had its say in the actions and decisions of the people. Socrates, Plato, and Aristotle all thought and wrote rather extensively on its effects, whether positive or negative.

The Athenians, like us, drew a distinction between what we now call the platonic love of friendship and erotic love. Socrates himself much preferred the love of friendship, according to Plato, which is, perhaps, the reason why we refer to that kind of love as Platonic. While Athenian men at the symposia got drunk and began to have sex with each other, Socrates preferred not to indulge in carnal pleasures, believing them to be too messy and distracting.

According to Plato's Socrates character, and perhaps the real Socrates as well, sex was supposed to be a means to an end—that of producing children who would grow up to be beautiful men and women. He didn't negate the powerful pleasure of sexual acts, however, but quite the opposite, in fact.

He was very concerned about not getting pulled into love's crazy trap, because he did not wish to be driven wild by it. He described a kiss as being like a bite from a scorpion with its poison. He said that beautiful boys were even more poisonous than scorpions, because while a scorpion needed to touch its subject to do harm, a beautiful boy could poison one with a glance from across the room.

Socrates was not indicative of the male norm. For Athenian men of his day, to be erotic and sexual was to be spiritual, and religion, as we know, played a huge role in the everyday life of the Athenian, regardless of citizenship status. Perhaps Socrates' lack of sexual indulgence was equated with the accusation of ungodliness.

Modern Pedophilia Versus Ancient Pederasty

It's hard to ignore the blatant mentions of erotic relationships between young boys and older men in the Greek philosophers' writings and teachings. It makes us squirm and brings to mind news stories of maladjusted middle aged men raping young children as the result of an unhealthy fixation or compensation.

Modern day pedophilia is usually defined as sexual activity with a prepubescent child between the ages of eight to eleven. The child in question, either male or female, is generally younger than thirteen and possesses a questionable understanding of what the sexual activities mean. Even if a child of this age consents to the sexual acts, it's doubtful that they have an understanding of what this consent encompasses. For obvious reasons, pedophilia is illegal in our culture, and pedophiles who indulge their fantasies do so in secret, because the relationship is socially inappropriate.

By contrast, ancient pederasty in Athens was meant to be both a sexual and educational relationship between a boy, who is generally between the ages of fourteen and twenty, and an older, respected man who is well established in the community. The boy's consent as well as his parents' consent is required for the relationship to begin. The older man must be reputable in the parents' eyes, because agreeing to the relationship makes him responsible for teaching the young boy in such a way that he will be ready to obtain his manhood, a point usually happening when his beard grows in—around when he is eighteen to twenty.

Unlike today's pedophiles, the relationship between a boy and an older man in classical Athens was not kept a secret. In fact, the older man had a huge personal stake in the sort of man the boy became. If the boy grew up to be a good man, then that was a point of pride for the older lover and teacher.

There were strict rules governing pederasty in ancient Greece. If the young boy acted as a prostitute, accepting money from older men in exchange for sexual acts, that kind of thing would follow the boy to manhood, potentially harming his future political career. Male prostitution wasn't illegal in Athens, but it was hugely looked down upon. A male citizen known to have prostituted himself in his youth had much to be ashamed of and little chance of securing a high office within the government system.

Sexual Orientation

The ancient Greeks didn't view sexuality in terms of homosexual, heterosexual, bisexual, transgender, or any of the common terms we use to define ourselves today. Some say that the Greeks were more sexually liberated than we are in that way, though the Socrates of Plato's writings insists that being a slave to ones sexual urges isn't freedom but a different sort of bondage.

Men could indulge in whatever sexual activity they desired, and it wasn't a point of shame as long as they were the ones doing the penetrating. An adult male citizen caught being penetrated by another man would be shamed, as he was allowing another man to treat him as an inferior. But an older man could penetrate a young man or a slave and feel no shame about that.

In the Greek eyes, marriage was for the production of children; extra marital affairs were for love. Marriage and love were in no way synonymous. A man always married a woman, even if he was sexually attracted to men, but he was free to have sex with whomever he pleased outside of his marriage, provided it wasn't with another man's wife.

Alcibiades

Alcibiades was the lover Socrates chose not to indulge, despite it being clear that he was attracted to him in a powerful way. In many ways, Alcibiades, the Athenian man known for his brash beauty, was a symbol of Athens in all of its potential and failure. He drank and partied and swayed off into the darkness of the city with lovers on each arm, even after declaring that he wished to learn from Socrates and improve his mind.

Alcibiades lusted after physical pleasures and did very little in his life with moderation. He walked the line between barbarity and earnest longing for wisdom, but even in death, he never overcame the pull for physical gratification to learn about the moderation that Socrates professed to be so important.

In many ways, to talk about Alcibiades is to talk about the city of Athens. Plato insinuates strongly that it is men like Alcibiades who are bringing Athens down through indulgence in the wrong type of love, a love that is burning, passionate, and destructive in its selfishness. Like Alcibiades, and not excluding the other Athenian men of the time, Athens was ever on a quest for a broader world perspective even while it aggressively pursued its own self interests.

CHAPTER NINETEEN: THE SORDID SEPARATE LIVES OF ATHENIAN WOMEN

Misogyny was not a new concept even as far back as ancient Greece, and Athens, by all accounts, was one of the most restrictive to women. Even in Sparta, the state of militaristic prowess and all things stereotypically masculine, the women were heavily encouraged to get naked and participate in their own public sporting events. Such a thing would have been utterly scandalous in Athens, where married women led lives that were almost completely separate from their male counterparts.

Like a modern day sit com, ancient literature from around that time period showed men griping about having to put up with women out of necessity. Countless examples can be found of male writers complaining about nagging wives, scary seductresses, and unpleasant female encounters.

Euripides wrote, "The counterfeit coin, woman, to curse the human race." Hippocrates a Greek medical expert said that when women began to menstruate, they were infectious in many different ways. Socrates made references to his wife, Xanthippe, who was said to have been quite the shrewish nag. Aristotle made comments about how if a man looked at a woman's eyes while she was menstruating, he could become infected by the air around her.

Women were not the sexual objects in ancient Greece that they are now. In stark contrast to today's society, men were the sexual objects in those days. Men had sex with their wives and mistresses out of necessity so that the population could increase, but they openly had sex with other men for their own pleasure and titillation. Sexual orientation wasn't a concept to them. So long as a man didn't allow himself to be penetrated by a man of lesser status, there was no shame in having sex with whomever he pleased, whether that was with another man, a male or female prostitute, or a young boy.

The same could not be said for women.

The sexual standard was not the same for women as it was for men. While men were under no obligation to keep sex within their marriages, women were under great obligation to have sexual relations only with their husbands. A married woman caught in adultery was lawfully required to be divorced and sent back to her father, or, in some circumstances, killed. This was true even if the woman was raped by a man who was not her husband.

A wife's sexual affair outside of her marriage was seen as dishonoring and shaming to her husband. Raping a man's wife in ancient Athens was kind of like smashing a man's car into a giant oak tree today; he would be angry about the deed and unable to fix it, so he'd get rid of it. In fact, if a man didn't divorce his wife after catching her with another man, then he could lose his citizenship.

It wasn't just the sexual standards that were different for women. Women were expected to perform a separate set of duties, which included training and managing the household slaves, caring for the household's sick, and visiting the tombs of the family's deceased to present offerings. If she was poor and had no slaves, she performed all of the household tasks herself. Sometimes she would be required to get a job to supplement the family's finances. Most jobs that were appropriate for women were as a wet nurse, midwife, or a trader at the market.

A woman's goal was to marry and have children. Her other goal was to keep herself away from men and out of the public spotlight, even going so far as to live in the rooms of the house that were the furthest from doors and windows. If a woman had to go out in the streets for any reason, it was best that she did so under the cover of night, and preferably if she was an older woman. Young women were seen as the most dangerous types of women.

The level of embarrassment a woman showed when she was in the presence of men was evidence of her family's respectability. The fact that no one knew her name was a badge of honor. Considering the fact that most of the women we hear about from that time period were mentioned in conjunction with a scandal or adulterous affair is evidence of that.

Women in classical Athens were expected to be silent, and as a result, these women will be silent for all of time.

Priestesses

In stark contrast to most Classical Athenian women, priestesses were highly visible in society and were given a great deal of honor and responsibility. A priestess was responsible for making sure that religious rituals in Athens ran smoothly. She was the one who managed the relationships of the city with all of the various gods.

A priestess was a wealthy woman who was expected to fund building projects, provide oil at the gymnasium, and donate animals for the sacrifices. She was, perhaps most importantly, given the large, unwieldy key to the temple sanctuaries. This was immensely important because the temple sanctuaries were like bank vaults for Athens' wealth.

Diotima of Mantinea was a priestess in Athens during Socrates' day, though some historians argue that Plato may have made her up for his dialogues. While this might be true to an extent, it's also true that Plato rarely, if ever, made up characters completely.

Diotima is known for her views on the meaning of love. In Plato's *Symposium*, which is a dialogue between dinner guests about the definition of real love, she said that love is a means by which one contemplates the divine. In other words, true human love always directs a person's attention toward spiritual things.

Prostitutes and Companions

Prostitution was both legal and common in classical Athens, but it's important to note the distinction between the statuses of different types of prostitutes. The *pornai* were the common prostitutes who usually had little or no education. Many of them were slaves who had no say over what they did with their bodies. The *hetaerae* were companions who often had an education and the freedom to choose which men they wanted to be with.

The most famous *hetaerae* was Aspasia from Miletus, who was said to have been well known in her day for her wit and wisdom. The very opposite of most women of her time, she was written into the literature instead of out of it. At some point before coming to Athens, she was educated, and, somehow, in a time when foreigners were the lowest of the low, she persevered, making it all the way to the top as Pericles' mistress.

Her status as a foreigner was both a drawback and a boon. The fact that she was a foreigner gave her an interesting freedom to speak and walk about in the daytime alongside men that few other women in Athens would dare risk. It was said that when she became Pericles' mistress, she rarely left his side, accompanying him at dinners and inserting her intelligence into lively debates. It's easy to imagine that she was the real reason behind Pericles' power. Socrates had respect for her, calling her his teacher in rhetoric and crediting her with composing Pericles' funeral speech herself.

She and Pericles were said to have been seen by their neighbors scandalously kissing each other in public every morning, and, despite public disgrace Pericles kept himself attached to her until he died with her at his side.

Religious Participation

Religion was, perhaps, the one thing women weren't expected to stand at the sidelines of being neither seen nor heard. They were responsible for mourning at funerals, making ritualistic sacrifices, and participating in religious festivals that were mandatory for women.

Every fourth year, chosen women would help make a new robe for the statue of Athena. On Athena's birthday, the noblemen's virgin daughters would be selected by the priestess of Athena to walk in a procession carrying sacred baskets. To not be selected was dishonorable to a young girl and might make her community assume that she was unchaste.

Women had a number of festivals that men weren't allowed to attend. One such festival was called Thesmophoria, during which the married female worshippers would insult each other, expose themselves, and carry phallic symbols around. Then they would slaughter many piglets and puppies, throw the corpses into pits, and bury them. Ten days later, they would dig up the partially decayed corpses and offer them as sacrifices to the goddess, Demeter.

Another festival was Brauronia, which celebrated the goddess Artemis. Every four years, young girls between the ages of eight and ten would march for two days from Athens to Brauron, where they would be kept for three to five years at a sort of boarding school. They lived as wild animals, participating in naked competitions and a ceremonial bear chase that may have involved being chased by real wild bears. The ceremony was undertaken to appease the goddess, Artemis, who had the power to kill women during childbirth. The girls were then taught how to be good Athenian housewives, and, around the age of twelve, with the spirit beaten out of them, they were marched back to Athens to find husbands.

It is within the realm of possibility that men were so nervous about being around women because of these violent religious festivals.

CONCLUSION: CHOOSING SIDES

Far from being a bunch of stuffy historical figures who had some outdated ideas, Socrates, Plato, and Aristotle were and still are some of the greatest thinkers of all time. Their different schools of thought are the shoulders that modern scholars continue to stand on to reach for even more elusive ideas.

Plato's worldview of idealism was in direct contrast to his student Aristotle's belief in realism. Plato believed that everything in the world is from the mind, and Aristotle argued that everything in the mind is from the world.

The evolution of these two schools of thought is fascinating, because descendants of either view seem to have followed a path leading to the conclusion that the other is correct. In other words, followers of Plato (and Socrates by proxy) start to believe Aristotle and vice versa.

Descendents of Plato's Worldview

Rene Descartes

Rene Descartes is widely hailed to be the father of modern philosophy. One of his profound epiphanies was realized when he decided to take all of the world's knowledge off of a metaphorical table in order to reconstruct it on his own. What he realized in doing this was that he could not reconstruct anything on his own. Descartes suggested that this was due to the fallibility of the human senses.

The senses are the way in which humans gather information about the world, and this process of gathering is flawed due to subjectivity and differences in acuteness. Descartes asserts that everything we think we know is actually varying levels of belief. The only fact that he could prove without a doubt was that he existed. This is where the phrase, "I think, therefore I am" came from.

In this vein, Descartes was a proponent of the Ontological argument. An example of this argument is that a square has four sides. That a square has four sides is an unshakable definition, which is fact. Similarly, that God has a definition necessitates the existence of God.

Another one of Descartes' axioms is that of Cartesian Dualism. Dualism refers to, what he believed were the two forms of matter that exist in the world. The first is physical matter, which could be the ebook device you hold in your hand, or the building that may or may not surround you. The second is "ghostly" matter, which would include the concepts of thought and souls.

In summary, Rene Descartes' central philosophy is that everything you believe you know may be wrong, and there is no way to verify its truth.

Gottfried Leibniz

Gottfried Leibniz belonged to a philosophical school of thought called rationalism, which suggested that thoughts and actions should be based on reason rather than emotion. Leibniz only ever wrote two treatises on philosophy, but his thoughts proved profound enough to be adopted as canon. Throughout his life, he worked primarily in mathematics and logic. But as was in fashion at the time, he worked to become a polymath (striving to be a master of multiple unrelated studies), including the liberal studies of philosophy. He was quite talented in this pursuit, having a law named after himself. Leibniz's Law is also known as the Identity of Indiscernibles.

The Identity of Indiscernibles suggests that if two separate entities have the same traits, they are the same entity. For instance, if two people have a nose, eyes, and a mouth, they are both people. The two people have separate identities, but they share an overarching category. Similarly, Leibniz also supported the philosophical principle of plenitude, which suggests that the universe contains all possible forms of existence. Leibniz intertwined the two concepts in his writings.

Immanuel Kant

Immanuel Kant was most concerned with ethics and what many consider to be moral gray areas. The most important tenet of his philosophy was deciding what is right and what is wrong. Kant's particular mode of thinking was the school of Deontology. This school of thought asserts that moral judgment is concerned with an act, rather than its consequences. For instance, murder is wrong. Even if it would prevent world war, the act itself is wrong, and therefore it should not be done. Because Kant wanted a concrete answer for what is right and wrong, he created the Categorical Imperative.

The Categorical Imperative puts forth that morality comes from rationality. Therefore anything considered rational is also moral. An objective morality can be derived from the same steps created through an objective rational thought. This process leaves no moral gray area. Something is either right or wrong based on objective traits. Context and circumstance do not apply in Kant's Categorical Imperative.

The actual fundamental traits of the Categorical Imperative are divided into three sections. The first is universality. Universality assumes that something is only socially acceptable if everyone in society could do it all of the time, without impinging upon others. The second section states that every human being should be treated as an end, rather than a means to an end. Therefore, one should not manipulate others in order to achieve something. The third and final section suggests that every individual should take on the role of total morality judge. In other words, each person must assume the responsibility of defining morality and call others out on poor behavior.

Descendents of Aristotle's Worldview

John Locke

John Locke was a philosopher whose work was later adapted to the political theories of the United States government. Locke is most well known for his concept of *tabula rasa*, meaning "blank slate." *Tabula rasa* asserts that all people are born without knowledge, and therefore, their brains are a blank slate on which memories and experiences can be written. Plato and his philosophical descendants were on the complete opposite side of the spectrum, believing that humans are born with all knowledge ready to be uncovered from within, or at least that they have some initial moral standards ingrained.

Tabula rasa assumes that there is no such concept as human nature; therefore, human nature is a taught behavior. Because Locke believed that everybody was born in a similar state, he suggested that all men are *created* equal. This exact statement was eventually written into the United States constitution. Locke, was thusly a proponent of the school of Empiricism, which suggests that all knowledge precedes observation.

Locke suggested that there are two forms of knowledge in the world—simple and complex. Simple knowledge is information that is derived directly from the world. For instance, knowing that a ball is round is simple knowledge. Complex knowledge is that which comes from a variety of simple knowledge sources. For instance, knowing that something is round, white, has dimples, and is traditionally hit with a metal stick means that it is a golf ball. A golf ball further suggests the game of golf, golf courses, country clubs, and so on. Locke believed that all of these complex concepts could be broken back down into facets of simple knowledge.

George Berkeley

George Berkeley suggested that objects do not exist, therefore the world does not exist. His school of thought was known as Immaterialism, and asserted that everything that is known through human observation is human perception. In other words, objects do not exist independently of the mind–the mind experiences and puts the object into a state of being. Berkeley's summary of this was, "to be, is to be perceived."

Following this axiom, Berkeley argued that dreams are just as real as reality, because dreams are perceived. Although one might believe that objects must exist independently of the self, because those objects can act upon the self (e.g. an oncoming train will end a person's life if they remain on the tracks as it comes), Berkeley–a catholic bishop–asserted that God kept all of humanity's perceptions in sync. In fact, he believed that God was the origin of all perception. This origin of perception, according to Berkeley, meant that God and man are not at all separated, because all of perception is within the mind, which does not exist without God.

David Hume

David Hume was a follower of John Locke, but pushed Locke's empiricism to a new extreme. Hume was a part of the Skepticism school of thought, which suggests that complete and pure knowledge is impossible to have, and that the real world, and its true features can never be discerned. Therefore, Hume believed, all reality and human experience exists only in the mind of the observer. He suggested that human experience is as close as humans will ever come to true knowledge.

On a related note, and sparked by his reading of Berkeley, Hume thought that sensory data retrieved through sight, sound, touch, smell, and taste were the only ways humans could acquire experience. This led to Hume's Bundle

Theory, which argues that features of objects are the only things that truly exist. In other words, objects are a conglomeration of features, but do not actually exist. An example would be a flower. A flower has petals, a stem, leaves, and a few other small parts. If the object does not have petals, a stem, leaves and the other small parts, it is no longer an object and does not exist.

Even more extreme was Hume's belief that there is no such thing as a self. He asserted that what humans believe themselves to be is merely a collection of sensory data. Though Hume believed in the nonexistence of self or objects, he still valued empiricism for its ability to recreate experiments and events.

These various schools of thought have both built off of and diverged from each other in some interesting ways. Perhaps the most interesting thing about all of this was the fact that, despite all of the disagreements between the schools of thought, philosophy has not changed in the fundamentals for over 2400 years.

We are as concerned with questions of our own existence, goodness, and virtue as the classical Athenian philosophers were. We still wonder what dreams mean, what our perception of reality really is and why it varies from another person's perception of reality, what is the best form of government, and whether our souls leave our bodies to go somewhere else after we die. We still ask questions about the will and the existence of God and wonder if anyone is keeping track of our ratio of good to bad deeds.

I earnestly hope that, at the very least, this book has made you more curious about exploring these questions, and I implore you to pick up Plato's dialogues or Aristotle's lecture notes to dig into the meat of their words for yourself.

Other books by author on paperback, Kindle and audio

Augustus: The Life And Times Of Rome's
Greatest Emperor

**Other history books by publisher Make
Profits Easy on Kindle, Paperback And
Audio**

**Hannibal Barca, The Greatest General:
The Meteoric Rise, Defeat, And
Destruction Of Rome's Fiercest Rival**

Description

In his book entitled Hannibal Barca, The
Greatest General: The Meteoric Rise, Defeat, and
Destruction of Rome's Fiercest Rival author
Barry Linton chronicles the adventures, myth,
and legacy of Hannibal Barca. Hannibal
accomplished many great successes, experienced
personal tragedies, and yet persevered through it
all. Nearly 2,200 years ago, he waged a 15 year
long campaign against the Romans called the
Second Punic War. He's a polarizing character in
history, and continues to be mysterious. Many
documents of his exploits were most likely
destroyed or altered by the conquering Romans,
but what remains of his story has been studied
by historians for over a thousand years. A

military genius, he survived in enemy lands and defeated nearly every army that ever assembled against him. His great strategic victories and stunning crossing of the Alps have been esteemed by modern-day military leaders. Hannibal is considered to be one of the most brilliant generals in history, fathering many strategies that would later be applied by leaders such as Napoleon.

Distinguished Generals have looked to his campaigns for guidance, such as Napoleon and George Patton. He led from the front, never asking his men to do what he would not. This book examines his life and his accomplishments. Follow along as we learn about his origins, beginning with his rise to power and ending with his eventual suicide. His life and legacy remains the subject of art, literature, as well as other mediums. Hannibal often faced numerically superior enemy forces, but through ingenuity and the loyalty of his men, he would win battle after battle against the Romans.

The Rise And Fall Of The Roman Empire: Life, Liberty, And The Death Of The Republic

Description

Arguably the greatest Empire to ever exist, Rome has indelibly left a significant mark on the modern world. The posthumous influence of the Roman Republic and Empire have no equal in all of history. Their varied culture, stunning art, brilliant philosophy, and towering architecture is embedded in our modern world. Roman innovation has left behind a legacy that has remained admired and emulated for over a thousand years. They built massive networks of roads before the birth of Christ. They constructed elaborate public sewer systems over 1,500 years before the United States became a Nation, and had networks of aqueducts bringing running water. Their tactics in battle are still studied by historians and military leaders of today. Their history is filled with great conflicts, compelling love stories, and the most treacherous of leaders. Hollywood has explored their culture time and again on the silver screen. Larger than life commanders like Julius Caesar would help shape their ultimate destiny.

In his book entitled The Rise and Fall of the Roman Empire: Life, Liberty, and the Death of the Republic author Barry Linton highlights and explains the significant struggles and contributions that have made Rome so well known. Join us as we explore the meteoric rise, monumental life, inevitable death, and eventual rebirth of Rome.

History's Greatest Military Commanders: The Brilliant Military Strategies Of Hannibal, Alexander The Great, Sun Tzu, Julius Caesar, Napoleon Bonaparte, And 30 Other Historical Commanders

Description

Armed conflict has produced many of the great leaders in human history. Some fought purely for glory, others waged war out of desperation, and even more were driven by a sense of duty. Every leader has human qualities that transcend time and culture. The lessons taught, tactics used, and losses suffered stand as a testament to their lives and accomplishments. In his book entitled History's Greatest Military Commanders author Barry Linton covers these leaders and great military commanders in fascinating detail, highlighting their distinguishable backgrounds and origins. Many were conquerors, some were innovators, and even others were liberators. One trait shared by all of these leaders is the willingness to adapt and overcome.

This book presents the true stories and struggles faced by these Commanders. Detailed battlefield plans are outlined, giving a step by step account of many important battles as well as information describing the context of each battle. The Commanders featured are drawn from all major periods of human history. Their achievements as well as their failures are highlighted, combined with the impact they had on the greater world and history. Follow along as we detail memorable historic greats such as:

Sun Tzu, Alexander the Great, Pyrrhus of Epirus, Darius the Third, Scipio Africanus, Hannibal Barca, Julius Caesar, Attila the Hun, Belisarius, Khalid Ibn Al-Walid, Charlemagne, Saladin, Genghis Khan, Timur, Edward the Black Prince, Suleiman the Magnificent, Oda Nobunaga, Yi Sun-sin, Hernan Cortes, Gustavus Adolphus, Duke of Marlborough, George Washington, Napoleon Bonaparte, Duke of Wellington, Horatio Nelson, Helmut von Moltke the Elder, Stonewall Jackson, Robert E. Lee, Ulysses S. Grant, Togo Heihachiro, John Monash, Erwin Rommel, Georgy Zhukov, Bernard Montgomery, George Patton.

BIBLIOGRAPHY

Barnes, J. (Ed.). (1995). *The Cambridge companion to Aristotle*. Cambridge: Cambridge University Press.

BRIA 26 1 Plato and Aristotle on Tyranny and the Rule of Law - Constitutional Rights Foundation. (n.d.). Retrieved October 17, 2015, from http://www.crf-usa.org/bill-of-rights-in-action/bria-26-1-plato-and-aristotle-on-tyranny-and-the-rule-of-law.html

Cartledge, P. (Ed.). (2002). *The Cambridge illustrated history of ancient Greece* (Pbk. ed.). Cambridge, U.K.: Cambridge University Press.

Descartes, R. (1998). *Descartes: Selected philosophical writings*. Cambridge: Cambridge University Press.

Garland, R. (1998). *Daily life of the ancient Greeks*. Westport, CT: Greenwood Press.

Gentry, J. (2009). *Ancient Pedophilia*. OH: Ohio State University.

Grube, G. (1992). *Republic*. Indianapolis, IN: Hackett Pub.

Hanson, V. (2005). *A war like no other: How the Athenians and Spartans fought the Peloponnesian War*. New York: Random House.

Hayes, B. (2012, April 21). Plato's Body, and Mine. Retrieved October 17, 2015, from http://www.nytimes.com/2012/04/22/op inion/sunday/platos-body-and-mine.html?_r=0

Hughes, B. (2011). *The hemlock cup: Socrates, Athens and the search for the good life*. New York: A.A. Knopf.

Hume, D., & Steinberg, E. (1993). *An enquiry concerning human understanding ; [with] A letter from a gentleman to his friend in Edinburgh ; [and] An abstract of a Treatise of human nature* (2nd ed.). Indianapolis, IN: Hackett Pub.

Linsley, A. (2010, January 18). Ethics Forum: Plato's Debt to Ancient Egypt. Retrieved October 17, 2015, from http://college-ethics.blogspot.com/2010/01/plato-and-ancient-egypt.html

Miller, Fred, "Aristotle's Political Theory", *The Stanford Encyclopedia of Philosophy* (Fall 2012 Edition), Edward N. Zalta (ed.), URL = <http://plato.stanford.edu/archives/fall2012/entries/aristotle-politics/>.

Nagy, G. (2015, March 27). The Last Words of Socrates at the Place Where He Died. Retrieved October 17, 2015, from http://classical-inquiries.chs.harvard.edu/the-last-words-of-socrates-at-the-place-where-he-died/

Nardo, D. (1997). *The trial of Socrates*. San Diego, CA: Lucent Books.

Peterman, J. (2000). *On Plato*. Belmont, CA: Wadsworth/Thomson Learning.

Philip of Macedon Philip II of Macedonia Biography. (2013). Retrieved October 17, 2015, from http://www.historyofmacedonia.org/AncientMacedonia/PhilipofMacedon.html

Powell, A., & Sheehan, S. (2003). *Cultural Atlas for Young People : Ancient Greece* (Rev. ed.). New York: Facts On File.

Plutarch. (n.d.). Alexander and Aristotle (Evelyn, Trans.). Retrieved October 17, 2015, from http://www.livius.org/aj-al/alexander/alexander_t04.html

Roberts, J., & Barrett, T. (2004). *The ancient Greek world*. Oxford, New York: Oxford University Press.

Rouse, W. (Trans.). (2008). *Great dialogues of Plato: Complete text of The republic, the apology, Crito, Phaedo, Ion, Meno, Symposium*. New York: Signet Classic.

Stone, I. (1988). *The trial of Socrates*. Boston: Little, Brown and Company.

Stoneman, R. (2004). *A traveller's history of Athens*. New York: Interlink Books.

Warner, R. (Trans.). (1954). *Thucydides: History of the Peloponnesian war*. London: Penguin.

Waterfield, R. (2004). *Athens: A history: From ancient ideal to modern city*. New York: Basic Books.

Printed in Great Britain
by Amazon